Cambridge Elements ≡

Elements in Psychology and Culture
edited by
Kenneth D. Keith
University of San Diego

PSYCHOLOGY AT THE INTERSECTIONS OF GENDER, FEMINISM, HISTORY, AND CULTURE

Alexandra Rutherford
York University, Toronto

CAMBRIDGE
UNIVERSITY PRESS

CAMBRIDGE
UNIVERSITY PRESS

University Printing House, Cambridge CB2 8BS, United Kingdom

One Liberty Plaza, 20th Floor, New York, NY 10006, USA

477 Williamstown Road, Port Melbourne, VIC 3207, Australia

314–321, 3rd Floor, Plot 3, Splendor Forum, Jasola District Centre,
New Delhi – 110025, India

79 Anson Road, #06–04/06, Singapore 079906

Cambridge University Press is part of the University of Cambridge.

It furthers the University's mission by disseminating knowledge in the pursuit of
education, learning, and research at the highest international levels of excellence.

www.cambridge.org
Information on this title: www.cambridge.org/9781108707145
DOI: 10.1017/9781108751094

First published 2021

A catalogue record for this publication is available from the British Library.

ISBN 978-1-108-70714-5 Paperback
ISSN 2515-3986 (online)
ISSN 2515-3943 (print)

Psychology at the Intersections of Gender, Feminism, History, and Culture

Elements in Psychology and Culture

DOI: 10.1017/9781108751094
First published online: January 2021

Alexandra Rutherford
York University, Toronto

Author for correspondence: Alexandra Rutherford, alexr@yorku.ca

Abstract: Psychologies of women and gender have developed – both institutionally and intellectually – within distinct social, cultural, historical, and political contexts. In many cases, feminism has played an important role in catalyzing disciplinary engagements with gender and culture as categories of analysis and sites of theorizing rather than solely as variables defining groups to be compared. The intersections of gender, feminism, history, and culture are explored with reference to psychology, first in the United States and then across three other national contexts. This exploration reveals the similarities and tensions between and among the approaches to studying culture and the approaches to studying gender that psychologists have employed. It also reveals the historically and culturally contingent nature of psychologies of women and gender and, by extension, of gender itself.

Keywords: gender, feminism, colonialism, intersectionality, globalization

ISBNs: 9781108707145 (PB), 9781108751094 (OC)
ISSNs: 2515-3986 (online), 2515-3943 (print)

Contents

1 Introduction

One of the most important tenets of postcolonial and multiracial feminist theory is that any understanding of gender must be based on an analysis of how categories such as "woman" or "women" come into being (and change) through particular relations of power defined by race, culture, class, history, and politics. That is, there is no unitary, homogenous, universal category of "woman" that is already constituted outside of these structures (hooks, 1981; Mohanty, 1988; Riley, 1988). That is, Culture itself is in gender, and gender is in culture. This invites a range of generative analytic possibilities for developing psychologies of gender. What are the relationships among gender, culture, and history? How has gender been socioculturally and historically constituted, and how has it functioned/does it function with respect to structures and relationships of power?

Some historians have been using gender, race, and class explicitly as categories of analysis since at least the 1980s (e.g., Scott, 1986). When gender is used as a category of *historical* analysis, the goal is to unpack how gender has functioned to materialize, configure, and enforce particular experiences, social organizations, and economic/political systems. Scott has argued that in reconstructing the past, historians must view sexual differentiation (as well as differentiation by race, class, ability, sexuality) as a primary way of signifying access to symbolic and material power.

Anthropologists (and some psychologists) have long studied the cultural constitution of sex-gender and sex-gender roles (e.g., Mead, 1935; Seward & Williamson, 1970). Sociologists, for their part, have studied how gender is generated and performed in social interaction within and across cultures and subcultures (e.g, West & Zimmerman, 1987). How have psychologists approached the relationship between gender and culture?

The answer to this question is complicated and to a large extent depends on the ontological, epistemological, and methodological assumptions underlying psychologists' conceptualizations of culture and of gender. That is, what psychologists *mean* by gender and what they *mean* by culture will influence their related views about how best to study the relationship. Because of this, I start this Element with a section that provides overviews of the conceptual and definitional development of the terms "gender" and "culture" in psychology. I then move to an examination of how gender has been studied in cross-cultural and cultural psychology, respectively. Next I move to how the field of the psychology of women and gender as it has developed in the United States has grappled with culture, including its own (perhaps underacknowledged) cultural embeddedness. Finally, I examine the history, status, and contours of the psychologies of women and gender in three national contexts other than the

US context to further demonstrate how these fields are socioculturally embedded, particularly in relation to local women's movements, political systems, and gender studies more generally. What do research priorities, topics, and approaches look like in these contexts, defined by their distinctive histories and social and political ideologies?

2 Gender and Culture in Psychology: Conceptual Issues

To unpack the conceptual issues and debates in psychology about the categories of "gender" and "culture," separately and together, would require volumes (e.g., Magnusson & Marecek, 2012). Here, I start with a selective review of the emergence of the category of gender in the social sciences, largely in the Global North, and to its trajectory in US psychology specifically. I note how it was originally differentiated from sex, how this differentiation has been approached in psychological research, and how, more recently, the strict differentiation between sex and gender has been challenged by feminist theorists and some psychologists. I then discuss the postcolonial critique of gender generated by feminist postcolonial scholars and Third-World feminists that has identified and disrupted the imposition of First-World perspectives on woman, gender, and feminism onto women living in other parts of the world. I conclude by reviewing decolonial feminist approaches that theorize the coloniality of gender.

I then move to the concept of culture to explore the various definitions and conceptual issues that have been discussed in psychology, noting the challenges of adopting and operationalizing some of these definitions in psychological research. The distinctions between cross-cultural and cultural psychology are reviewed, and critiques of these fields from a decolonizing perspective are outlined.

2.1 Unpacking Gender in Psychology

Gender operates in psychology on multiple, dynamically interacting levels. Psychologists have genders; they work in cultures saturated with various beliefs about gender; they take gender as an object of direct study (i.e., they construct theories about the very nature of gender, how it develops, and how it functions); and they conduct empirical studies to identify differences and similarities among genders. These studies often have intended and unintended social repercussions, thus feeding directly back into the cultures from which they originate. Drawing on the notion of the science/gender system as outlined by feminist scholars such as Evelyn Fox Keller (Keller, 1985) it is clear that psychology as a discipline and a body of knowledge both draws on and reproduces (and only occasionally disrupts) the gender system (see Rutherford, 2015, 2020; Rutherford, Vaughn-Johnson, & Rodkey, 2015).

Given this, how have psychologists conceptualized gender and approached it epistemologically, theoretically, and methodologically? How has the contemporary notion of gender as distinct from, but in relation to, biological sex developed and been taken into account in psychological studies? This section provides a selective conceptual history of the evolution of gender in psychology, from an emphasis on sex roles to gender identity and to gender as process, concluding with an examination of the gender/power relationship as articulated in postcolonial and decolonial critique.

2.1.1 From Sex Roles to Gender

The emergence of the modern concept of gender in the US-based social sciences is often partially attributed to the work of cultural anthropologist Margaret Mead. Mead examined the cultural construction of sex roles across different "primitive" societies in New Guinea in the early 1930s (Mead, 1935). By observing the "temperaments" and attendant social roles of men and women of the Arapesh, Mundugumor, and Tchambuli tribes, Mead concluded that in each case the patterns were dissimilar from each other and from what was then typical of American society. Among the Arapesh, for example, both men and women occupied what Mead called the maternal or feminine sex role and temperament, while among the Mundugumor both men and women displayed a temperament and role that, in the United States, would be described as a rather violent and undisciplined masculinity. The Tchambuli, by contrast, did display sex role differentiation, but it was the inverse of the stereotypical American case. Tchambuli women were more often dominant, impersonal, and managerial, and Tchambuli men were less responsible and more emotionally dependent. Although Mead did not use the term "gender," she clearly distinguished the expression of femininity and masculinity from sex itself, concluding that these temperaments and roles were cultural constructions unlinked to biological sex.

Building on Mead's ideas but adopting an evolutionary perspective, US psychologist Georgene Seward published *Sex and the Social Order* in 1946 (Seward, 1946). This book, catalyzed by the immediate post-WWII context in which traditional sex roles had (at least temporarily) been challenged, Seward surveyed the sexual behaviors and social arrangements in animal species from fish to apes. She noted that these were quite flexible within and between species, with sex-role differentiation becoming more subject to cultural regulation the further one ascended up the phylogenetic scale. Building on this observation, she asked why we had come to so rigidly assign certain social roles to biological sex in human societies. She was motivated to reimagine this sex-typed social order so that women and men were not constrained by traditional sex roles. Again, without using the language of gender, Seward was clearly decoupling social and cultural processes from biological sex (see also Rutherford, 2017).

In the same year as Seward's treatise, Austrian sociologist Viola Klein published *The Feminine Character: History of an Ideology* (Klein, 1946) in which she traced ideas about femininity and their association with the female sex throughout history and culture. Her conclusion that the feminine character is socially created and culturally and historically contingent was consistent with later notions of gender. Another early articulation of the cultural construction of womanhood was offered by French philosopher Simone de Beauvoir in her classic book *The Second Sex* (de Beauvoir, 1949), in which she famously cast the creation of woman as a result of her positioning as the "other" in relation to man. Woman is not born but becomes a woman through the process of subordination to, and differentiation from, the default sex that is man. All of these scholars were theorizing gender, without using the term, as the process whereby certain traits, social roles, and social arrangements accrue to biological sex (see also Tarrant, 2006).

2.1.2 Emergence of the Term "Gender"

The explicit use of the term "gender" in contrast to "sex role" (at least in the academic social sciences) arose in a particular historical and psycho-medical context. In the 1950s, US psychologist John Money was working in a clinic at Johns Hopkins University to develop a protocol for the "treatment" of infants identified as intersex. Gender studies scholar David Rubin has argued that "Intersex literally gave birth to gender" (Rubin, 2012, p. 904). By this Rubin means that the term "gender" was originally invented in the context of Money's attempts to make intelligible, organize, and ultimately manage bodies that presented as sexually ambiguous because of incomplete or inconsistent (according to binary conceptualizations) gonadal, hormonal, genital, or chromosomal sex in a cultural context that disallowed anything other than dimorphous sex (i.e., that one must be either exclusively male or exclusively female).

In his work, Money became dissatisfied with the terminology being used to refer to the "manliness" or "womanliness" of people born with "indeterminate" sex status and began to search for a new term. He felt that the term "sex" itself was imprecise because it referred both to the biological status of the body and to the act of having sex. The terms "sexual identity" and "sex role," he felt, were similarly inexact. Money wanted language to refer to a person's outlook, demeanor, orientation (including but not limited to their sexual orientation), and presentation as masculine or feminine. He chose gender as this term, often using "gender" and "gender role" interchangeably in his early work. Money defined gender role as "the overall degree of masculinity and or femininity that is privately experienced and publicly manifested in infancy, childhood, and adulthood, and that usually though not invariably correlates with the anatomy of the organs of procreation" (Money, 1995, pp. 18–19). Notably, Money believed that gender roles were learned and therefore not innately biologically sex-linked, but he nonetheless felt that gender roles and sex should align. This was the goal of his clinical protocol: to make an early decision, based on the viability of certain external sexual organs, whether a "sexually indeterminant" infant should be assigned biological maleness or femaleness and to instantiate the appropriate (congruent) gender role through strict socialization over the course of development.

Although Money introduced the term "gender," psychiatrist Robert Stoller's articulation of gender *identity* as being separate from biological sex even more forcefully distinguished the two (Stoller, 1968). Stoller was a psychoanalyst who formed the Gender Identity Project at the University of California Los Angeles Medical School in the late 1950s in order to study what was then called "transsexualism." In working with patients whose sense of themselves as male or female did not match the biological sex they were assigned at birth, Stoller proposed the term "gender identity" as the psychological self-understanding and awareness of oneself as male or female, whereas gender *role* was the awareness of the behavioral and social expectations associated with belonging to a gender. According to Germon (2009), this allowed Stoller to separate the psychological (gender identity) from the cultural (gender role) and to then focus on the psychological, which was congruent with his training as a psychoanalyst and with his clinical focus. Focusing on gender identity also allowed him to free gender from the biological trappings of sex and thus to conceptualize transsexualism as a "mismatch" between assigned sex and gender identity (for histories of the psy-disciplines' involvement in regulating transgender experience, see Meyerowitz, 2002; Riggs et al., 2019; Stryker, 2008).

Stoller's conceptual separation of gender identity and role from biological sex became highly useful for subsequent feminist theorizing in psychology. By drawing a clear line between sex as a biological and corporeal phenomenon and gender as a psychological and social one, it became possible for feminist psychologists to analyze social and political inequalities between men and women in terms that were free of the biological determinism that had been used so pervasively to justify sex differences earlier in the century. As Viveras-Vigoya (2016) has written, "By demonstrating that the biological and the social belonged to distinct domains, and that social inequalities on the grounds of sex were not 'natural,' feminist works sought to disrupt notions that power inequalities between men and women derived from anatomical differences" (p. 854).

In some respects, this fueled an incredibly productive line of thinking about gender that was completely untethered from its association with a corporeal body. Gender – and gendering – could be thought of as a social and cultural process that was continuously unfolding and changing. This process could then be subjected to analysis and interrogation for the ways it was used to enforce relations of power. In other respects, however, the untethering of gender from the body set up the overly simplistic dichotomy of "sex equals biology" and "gender equals culture," a dichotomy that has proven difficult to sustain (a topic to which we will return; see Grosz, 1994; Wilson, 2004).

With gender thus defined as a psychological experience and a social expression that is not given at birth but that develops and is reinforced in particular sociohistorical and cultural contexts, scholars began to explore a range of questions. How does gender take on different meanings and expressions? How do bodies become gendered and how does gender function to regulate access to power and status? How does gender interact with other social formations such as race/ethnicity, class, and sexual orientation to affect people's experiences in the world?

2.1.3 Gender Takes Hold in US Psychology

In 1978, psychologists Suzanne Kessler and Wendy McKenna continued the "denaturalization" project by undertaking an ethnographic analysis of how gender is established, expressed, and maintained. In their groundbreaking study *Gender: An Ethnomethodological Approach*, they immersed themselves in the lives of members of the transgender community to illuminate the day-to-day processes through which members of this community went about expressing and enacting their desired genders. As Kessler and McKenna showed, acquiring and maintaining a gender involved following strict rules requiring, at least for a time, constant vigilance in order to successfully "pass" as a man or a woman (e.g., maintaining "proper" talk, gestures, responses, gait, etc.). Although the "rules" of gender were put into stark relief due to the challenges faced by transgender people in acquiring a new, socially accepted gender, these rules also reveal the myriad ways gender is performed by virtually everyone, all the time, to maintain the "natural" appearance of masculinity and femininity (Kessler & McKenna, 1978; for a historical analysis of racial "passing" see Hobbs, 2014).

In 1979, feminist psychologist Rhoda Unger published a widely read article "Toward a redefinition of sex and gender" in which she defined sex as a stimulus variable that, as used in psychological research, reflected one's presumed biological maleness or femaleness. Gender, by contrast, was the socially constructed sets of characteristics, qualities, and traits associated with maleness or femaleness. She argued that the focus on sex differences that had characterized so much of psychological research should be abandoned for at least three reasons: (1) Questions about sex differences usually took the male as the standard and examined women's deviation from this standard as a problem and, as such, were fundamentally not very feminist questions; (2) these studies diverted attention from the fact that the sexes shared many more similarities than differences; and (3) they obscured consideration of the social constraints and conditions that regulated gender (Unger, 1979). Despite Unger's call for an abandonment of sex differences research, this research has continued relatively unabated. It is now often called "gender differences research" with gender simply standing in as the stimulus variable. Cleary, Unger's call was for a different research paradigm altogether based on viewing gender as a process that is socially and culturally mediated. This orientation to gender has been taken up by many feminist psychologists, but not all.

Further to this, in 1987 sociologists Candace West and Don Zimmerman's formulation of "doing gender" also highlighted that gender is enacted continuously in everyday social interactions (West & Zimmerman, 1987). Their formulation moved explicitly beyond theories of gender socialization, which posited that girls and boys, by the time they reach a certain age, have internalized a learned set of gendered norms that will remain relatively invariant throughout their lives. Doing gender, they argued, was a dynamic, ongoing, continuous aspect of everyday life.

On the basis of this work, and in tandem with postmodern critiques of psychology more generally (which tend to emphasize the roles of social interaction, language, and discourse in the constitution of psychological categories, see Gavey, 1989; Gergen, 2001), gender moved beyond the status of a variable that divides the world (or the research sample) into male, female, or other and became a category of analysis in and of itself. Notably, feminist philosopher Judith Butler's work on gender, which has been foundational to queer theory, has also been drawn upon by some feminist psychologists to recognize the role that language and action play in producing and reproducing gender, and specifically the gender binary. Butler argues that gender, and indeed the (sexed) subject who performs gender, has no a priori status outside language. Gender is not simply an agreed-upon system of meanings imposed onto bodies with a predetermined sex; rather, gender is the very apparatus by which the sexes themselves are produced. As Rubin (2012) has put it, according to Butler, gender is "a generative technology that naturalizes the illusion of a prediscursive sex" (p. 890). Gender, in

Butler's formulation, is an ongoing process; the gender system is continuously being produced and reproduced through the very acts that are usually assumed to merely express it. This is what is meant by gender as *performative*.

Further, Butler contends that the maintenance of the *binaries* of sex and gender and their correspondence (male sex = masculine gender, female sex = feminine gender) is being constantly reinforced (and thus made to appear natural) by the "restricting frames of masculinist domination and compulsory heterosexuality" (Butler, 1990, p. 141). That is, this process is constantly taking place within frames that limit its expression and possibility. Butler's work troubles the binary framework, exhorting readers to examine other possibilities, transgress gender norms, and create room and viability for a range of gender expressions.

This perspective has been taken up by critical feminist psychologists who focus on the roles of discourse and language in producing and regulating gender and gender relations (for an overview see Gavey, 1989). In this view, discourse is a broad term defined as "a way of constituting meaning which is specific to particular groups, cultures, and historical periods and is always changing" (Gavey, 1989, p. 464). Language does not simply reflect the underlying "truth" of a participant's experience; accounts of experience are themselves produced within sets of discourses that make certain accounts of experience more intelligible than others and that, in turn, reinforce and reproduce the discourses in which they are embedded. Feminist discursive psychologists focus on gendered dimensions of language and experience, and how these both reflect and reproduce gendered power relations and social inequities. Notably, discursive approaches to gender have been taken up more extensively by scholars in the United Kingdom, Australia, New Zealand, and to some degree Canada, than in the United States. A discursive approach necessarily attends to culture and historical period, and does not assume that discourses of gender are universal or ahistorical, though there may be similarities across cultures.

Although the conceptual distinction between (biological) sex and (sociocultural) gender has been useful to feminist theory and to feminist psychology, this distinction is not as straightforward as it might seem and has been difficult to maintain. Some feminist science studies scholars have pointed out that the biology of sex is not impervious to the influence of cultural conceptions of gender. That is, biological (genetic, hormonal, reproductive) theories are themselves suffused with cultural gender conceptions (Findlay, 1995; Martin, 1991; Oudshoorn, 1994; Richardson, 2013). Others argue that the emergence of sexual dimorphism, which insists that every "normal" – that is, medically and culturally intelligible – body is either unambiguously male or unambiguously female, is itself a specific cultural and historical production (Laqueur, 1990). It obscures the actual biological variability of sex categories (Fausto-Sterling, 2000) and the fact that gendered experiences feed back to influence the biology of sex (Fausto-Sterling, 2012).

Given the interdependence of sex and gender, some theorists, including some feminist psychologists, prefer to use the term sex/gender or gender/sex to signal this inseparability and to break down the assumption that one can neatly parse (biological) sex from (cultural, socialized) gender (see Hyde et al., 2019). Van Anders (2015) has argued compellingly that gender/sex is necessary to capture the myriad social locations and identities where gender and sex cannot be meaningfully – or logically – disentangled.

2.1.4 Feminist Postcolonial and Decolonial Critiques

So far, this review of the conceptual development of gender in psychology has focused on the work of scholars and psychologists largely in the United States (see also Rutherford, 2019). Starting in the 1970s, subfields of psychology that explicitly embraced feminist approaches to analyzing gender and gender relations were established, intellectually and institutionally, in the United States and in many other national contexts (see Rutherford, Capdevila, Undurti, & Palmary, 2011). Along with the emergence and evolution of feminist psychologies were, of course, developments in feminist theory more generally that would forcefully bring together considerations of gender and culture through a consideration of the impact of histories of colonization and the ongoing effects of colonialism. Postcolonial and decolonial feminist critique have influenced feminist psychology, but unevenly.

Starting in the late 1980s, feminist scholars began to critique Western feminism and Western theories of gender for their tendency to stereotype and "other" the experiences of non-Western women. Postcolonial feminist scholars from the Global South, for example, highlighted how Western feminist scholars have theorized Third World women as a monolithic, homogenous category that is already structured prior to any entry into social relations; namely, they are uniformly cast as uneducated, poor, powerless victims. This limits any consideration of the complexity of Third-World women's lives and identities (a complexity that First-World women are presumed to have), their potential agency, and – importantly – the processes through which their lives and identities are constituted in and through legal, economic, religious, social, and family structures.

Postcolonial scholar Gayatri Spivak, in her analysis of nineteenth-century British literature, critiqued Western feminism for failing to see how its own construction of the (valorized) female subject (e.g., the eponymous protagonist in the novel *Jane Eyre*) depends on a collusion with colonialism and the "worlding" of the Third World as a distant place whose cultural and literary heritage lie in wait for discovery and translation (Spivak, 1985). In her classic essay "Can the subaltern speak?" Spivak (1988) specifically called out how the discursive construction of the Third-World woman in Western scholarship effectively silenced her, performing an act of ventriloquism that reinscribed the dominance of the West over the rest as a form of epistemic violence. As Mendoza (2016) has put it, Spivak suggested that "every attempt to represent the subaltern woman was a way of asserting the West's superiority over the non-West," (p. 109) a form of colonizing the subaltern experience.

Chandra Talpade-Mohanty, in her article "Under Western eyes" (1988), extended this critique, demonstrating how dichotomous constructions of First-World and Third-World women homogenized both categories but specifically positioned Third-World women as abject others in need of the redemptive powers of their First-World counterparts and of Western feminism (Mohanty in turn has been critiqued for stereotyping Western feminism as homogenous). Other postcolonial feminists have taken up explicitly intersectional analyses to examine how gender, race, sexuality, and nationality structure power in colonial contexts (e.g., McClintock, 1995; Stoler, 2002).

In contrast to postcolonial theorists, whose original work drew largely from the context of the colonization of South Asia by the British and the French, decolonial theorists have drawn on the relatively longer history of the Spanish and Portuguese colonization of the Americas, which began in the sixteenth century and ended in the nineteenth century. They turn their focus away from the subaltern, who is silenced by the West, to the potential power of the subaltern voice, specifically the voices of indigenous peoples who have variously resisted and challenged colonization for centuries. In part because of the longer time span on which they draw, decolonial scholars also see capitalism – not as preexisting colonialism – but as dependent on it for its emergence and maintenance. Namely, capitalism required, and requires, the internal conditions of the colony to realize itself.

Given that capitalist systems demand that the freedom of some be realized and enacted through the subordination of others, there always exists a coloniality of power. Coloniality thus outlives explicit colonization and is deeply implicated in the formation of capitalist modernity. Coloniality also continues to permeate systems of knowledge production, such that knowledge produced by former colonizers continues to be regarded as superior to that of the formerly colonized and is thus imposed as hegemonic knowledge. This produces the ongoing epistemicide of indigenous knowledge systems and reproduces the ongoing coloniality of knowledge. Finally, coloniality extends to the psyche and social relations, producing what Nelson Maldonado-Torres calls the "coloniality of Being" (Maldonado-Torres, 2007). The coloniality of being is constituted by ways of thinking, feeling, and experiencing that are associated with European global domination and that displace (often violently) other ways of being (see Adams, Estrada-Villalta, & Ordonez, 2018) . Preeminent decolonial scholar Walter Mignolo refers to this as the "darker side" of Western modernity (Mignolo, 2011) and uses the coupling of modernity/coloniality as a central analytic concept.

A foundational articulation of feminist decolonial theory is the work of Chicana feminist Gloria Anzaldua, whose semiautobiographical work *Borderlands/La Frontera: The New Mestiza* (Anzaldua, 1987) put forth the concept of mestiza consciousness and pensamiento fronterizo, or border thinking. Born and raised in Texas near the US-Mexico border, Anzaldua writes powerfully of the impact of living in the borderlands, in a border culture:

> The U.S.-Mexican border es *una herida abierta* where the Third World grates against the first and bleeds. And before a scab forms it hemorrhages again, the lifeblood of two worlds merging to form a third country – a border culture. Borders are set up to define the places that are safe and unsafe, to distinguish *us* from *them*. A border is a dividing line, a narrow strip along a steep edge. A borderland is a vague and undetermined place created by the emotional residue of an unnatural boundary. It is in a constant state of transition. (Anzaldua, 1987, p. 25)

The borderlands is a place – both literal and symbolic – that is fraught with contradictions, dualisms, and transitions. Forged in the borderlands, mestiza consciousness is a form of consciousness that is subversive, that breaks down either/or constructions and binary categories of race, gender, sexuality, language, geography, and religion to produce new angles of vision. Pensamiento fronterizo, or border thinking, is a form of thinking that characterizes mestiza consciousness. In her work, Anzaldua deconstructs the impact of colonialism and patriarchy on the Chicana psyche to articulate new forms of consciousness that expand personal, social, and political possibilities.

More recently, feminist decolonial scholar Maria Lugones has proposed (not uncontroversially) that heteronormativity and the binary gender system are imbricated with colonialism to produce a coloniality of gender. She argues that "gender" did not exist in indigenous societies as a relation or structure of power before colonization. Rather, gender is a completely colonial construct imposed by European colonizers onto indigenous societies with violent intent and consequences. As Mendoza (2016) has put it, Lugones argues that "In the process of colonization, women and men in the colony were both racialized and sexualized as gender was deployed as a powerful tool to destroy the social relations of the colonized by dividing men and women from each other and creating antagonisms between them" (p. 116). Male sexual violence against indigenous women, both by the colonizers and by indigenous men who were forced to surrender women into concubinage, Lugones argues, was used to subjugate and break down both indigenous men and women in order to secure European domination. Lugones calls this the dark side of the modern colonial/gender system.

In her 2010 essay "Toward Decolonial Feminism," Lugones advances this idea even further by proposing that the gender system forced onto indigenous societies by European colonizers differed from their own, more "advanced" European gender system. As she argues, because complete dehumanization of the colonized is the goal of colonization, indigenous people were cast as subhuman "beasts of burden" who lacked "civilized" gender. That is, while European women were subjugated to European men in the colonies because they, by virtue of their reproductive function, were also closer to nature, they still had culture. Indigenous men and women were dehumanized, stripped of culture, and therefore were constructed as having biological sex differentiation but not a complex gender system. As she put it:

> Under the imposed gender framework, the bourgeois white Europeans were civilized; they were fully human. The hierarchical dichotomy as a mark of the human also became a normative tool to damn the colonized. The behaviors of the colonized and their personalities/souls were judged as bestial and thus non-gendered, promiscuous, grotesquely sexual, and sinful. (Lugones, 2010, p. 743)

Other decolonial feminist scholars, including indigenous feminists, have complicated Lugones' earlier claim that indigenous societies had no gender system prior to colonization and that colonization completely destroyed extant gender systems. Nonetheless, Lugones' work does highlight how gender operates according to the genocidal logic of the coloniality of power that is well substantiated by historical documentation and embedded in contemporary legal and policy frameworks, frameworks that, for example, allow the ongoing sterilization and murder of indigenous women.

In US feminist psychology, there has been little uptake of decolonial theory specifically, with few exceptions (which I will discuss further, e.g., Kurtiş & Adams, 2015). The more general need for decolonizing approaches has, however, received some attention. For example, the influential work of Linda Tuwahi-Smith on decolonizing methodologies (Smith, 1999) has been heeded by some US feminist psychologists (e.g., Fine, 2018). Additionally, there has been ample critique by US women of color feminists of the colonizing effects of theory developed by and for White women and the need for multiracial and multicultural feminist theory that is based on the different histories, experiences, and relationships of power that affect women of color (Hurtado, 1997).

Perhaps not unsurprisingly, the need to decolonize psychology has begun to make some impact on feminist psychologies outside the United States. Most notably, in 2020 a special issue of the international journal *Feminism & Psychology* was devoted to "feminisms and decolonising psychology" (see Macleod, Bhatia, & Liu, 2020). Feminist scholars in South Africa, where the project of decolonizing psychology has been actively pursued, have also contributed prominently to this project (e.g., Boonzaier, Kessi, & Ravn, 2019; Macleod, Masuko, & Feltham-King, 2019).

2.1.5 Summary

This section has outlined how gender came to acquire its distinct conceptual meaning as a socioculturally and historically constituted category that is dynamic, enacted, and takes on different functions over time and place. The work of postcolonial and decolonial scholars has emphasized that gender itself is used to enforce or deny culture to certain groups and that gender is used to enforce relations of power. In psychology, feminist psychologists who study gender in this way often see gender and culture as inseparable – gender is in culture, and culture is in gender. Given this, how does the concept of "culture," as it is taken up in psychology, relate to these ideas about gender? In the Section 2.2 I take a closer look at how "culture" has been conceptualized and defined by psychologists before merging the considerations of gender and culture.

2.2 Unpacking Culture

It is an understatement to note that "culture" is a complicated term with multiple meanings, both in psychology and as it is used colloquially. As Magnusson and Marecek (2012) note, "There are few terms in the social sciences that have been given so many, and such diverse meanings, as 'culture'" (p. 20). In this section I summarize how psychologists have conceptualized culture in the context of their theoretical and empirical investigations.

To simplify, since the 1960s two dominant schools of thought have coalesced on this topic, namely, the cross-cultural (sometimes called cultural-comparative) versus cultural perspectives. These approaches are embedded in very different assumptions about the relationship between culture and human nature and how best to study this relationship. I will review the ontological and epistemological bases of each of these two schools to demonstrate how they have come to think of and study culture in such distinct ways.

Additionally, some psychologists have developed a meta-critique of culture as it has been conceptualized in psychology. This critique challenges the tendency to view culture as relatively bounded, homogeneous, and static, especially in an era of intense and continuous global communication, migration, and diaspora. It also challenges the isomorphism of culture with nation-state and points out how histories of colonization shape both political boundaries and experiences of self and identity in ways that fracture any straightforward treatment of "culture." If culture itself is an ongoing and dynamic *process* of meaning making continuously shaped by these forces, rather than a static set of shared meanings/values equated with specific national boundaries, what kinds of psychological questions result?

2.2.1 Cross-Cultural versus Cultural Psychology

The modern academic study of culture has traditionally been the purview of anthropology (for a critical history of the study of culture in anthropology, see Kuper 1999). However, starting in about the 1960s in the US context, psychologists interested in how psychological phenomena vary across cultures began to join together to establish an identifiable subdiscipline called cross-cultural psychology. These scholars were concerned with the increasingly Western emphasis of mainstream psychology and sought to correct the ethnocentrism of their discipline. To signal the institutional inauguration of this field, the *Journal of Cross-Cultural Psychology* made its debut in 1970. A number of other important conferences, handbooks, and research programs followed (for overviews, see Kashima & Gelfand, 2012; Lonner, 2013; Tonks, 2014).

Scholars in the cross-cultural tradition (sometimes referred to as the cultural-comparative approach) generally adhere to a positivist philosophy of science. They use objective observation and measurement of psychological variables to establish causal explanations for similarities and differences across cultures. They share the goal of developing universal laws, as well as explaining cultural variations (similarities and differences) in psychological characteristics and measurements on standardized tests (Keith, 2008; Tonks, 2014). Cross-cultural psychologists often invoke figures such as W. H. R. Rivers, Francis Galton, and Frederic Bartlett as their historical antecedents. These were scholars who administered tests of basic psychological and sensory processes across cultures.

The nature of culture itself, in the cross-cultural approach, tends to be accorded the status of a variable, defined, most generally, as the shared set of meanings, values, beliefs, and practices that define a relatively bounded group. This definition makes possible both the comparisons of different cultures and the deployment of culture as a relatively well-defined independent variable. A classic example would be comparing research participants from Eastern

(Asian) versus Western (US) cultures on measures of independence versus interdependence (Markus & Kitayama, 1991). Another example would be taking a psychological test developed in one context (such as the test of the Big Five personality traits developed in the United States) to see if its factor structure replicates across cultures (McCrae et al., 1998). In much cross-cultural research, "cultures" are defined by, and located within, national boundaries, that is, in many cases, a country (or sometimes a region) is a culture.

Cultural psychology, by contrast, emerged institutionally a little bit later than its cross-cultural cousin and, in some respects, as a response to it. In the mid-1980s, Richard Shweder began criticizing cross-cultural psychology for its focus on establishing universality rather than understanding cultural meaning (Shweder, 1984, 1991). Cultural psychologists, as he (and others) outlined, study the cultural and historical constitution of human subjectivity itself. As Slunecko and Wieser (2014) have put it, the "dynamic and reciprocal co-constitution of culture and psyche is the pivotal premise of cultural psychology" (p. 348). In 1995 Jan Vaalsiner established the journal *Culture & Psychology* as an outlet for research based on these tenets.

To study the co-constitution of culture and psyche, cultural psychologists generally seek to understand the uniqueness (rather than the universality) of this process and its products. Scholars in this tradition invoke Wilhelm Wundt, Giambattisa Vico, and Lev Vygotsky as some of their intellectual forebears. In cultural psychology, psychological phenomena are, ontologically speaking, "relational processes unfolding with and via others, as well as through more enduring cultural symbols, traditions, and the power relations within society" (Ellis & Stam, 2015, p. 301). That is, to study psychology is to study how different constellations of social, political, and cultural contexts come to "make up" psychological life and how these change over the course of an individual's life span and across historical time.

Cultural psychologists do not see the individual as separate from culture, but rather bound up in it, and thus reject the individualist ontology and epistemology of cross-cultural psychology. Theory and method too are bound up together, and although there is no single set of methods in cultural psychology, researchers tend to favor qualitative approaches that allow for the study of individuals-in-culture and their processes of meaning making and performance. Humans are understood to be reflexive meaning makers and to move among different social groups and sets of cultural meanings. Specific methods suited to exploring these processes, such as field research, group discussion, discourse analysis, narrative approaches, and analysis of cultural artifacts, are all in play (Slunecko & Wieser, 2014). Cultural psychology thus holds understanding and the interpretation of meaning, rather than explanation, as its primary epistemological and methodological aims. That said, within cultural psychology different theorists emphasize different aspects of this framework.

2.2.2 Culture, Power, Globalization, and Decolonization

Psychology's theorization and study of culture, in both cross-cultural and cultural psychology traditions, has been largely unaffected by postcolonial and decolonial critiques (for recent exceptions, see Adams & Salter, 2007, Adams et al., 2012; Adams et al. 2018; Bhatia, 2007; 2018; Bhatia & Ram, 2001; Grabe & Dutt, 2015; Kurtiş & Adams, 2015; Moane, 1999). These critiques encompass a number of shared elements. First, they highlight the often-implicit elision of culture with nation, a presumed isomorphism that flattens the differences among groups within nations, obscures the histories of colonization responsible for the boundaries of particular nation-states and the uneven experiences within it, and ignores the ongoing reinscription of colonial power relations through structural racism and the differential effects of globalization. Second, they explicitly foreground the relationships of power – historic and ongoing – in which any understanding and experience of culture is embedded, including how these relationships unfold *within* current nation-states and between the so-called Global North and the Global South. Third, and following from this, these critiques reject any static notion of culture or cultural identity in favor of conceptualizations that emphasize how people move among/in cultures through migration, immigration, and the formation of diasporic communities, moves that require navigating ongoing relationships of domination and subjugation. This results in multiple, complex, and shifting forms of cultural "identities."

In the early 1990s, postcolonial scholar Homi Bhabha (e.g., Bhabha, 1994) theorized the effects of colonization on the formation of selfhood by suggesting a number of ways colonized groups respond to and interact with ongoing processes of colonization. Influential to critical cultural psychologists, he elaborated the notion of hybridization. Hybridization refers to the processes through which people under colonization, or its ongoing manifestations in globalization, forge new forms of selfhood in times of change or cultural disruption. As critical cultural psychologist Sunil Bhatia (2018) writes: "The cultural hybridity manifested in colonial times or in globalization reveals a movement between sameness and difference, ambivalence and appropriation, and continuity and discontinuity" (p. 16). In its original context, part of Bhabha's intent was to challenge top-down conceptualizations of the flow of power to reveal the often subversive ways colonized subjects refigure their identities and experiences. Postcolonially, these processes continue to unfold through both globalization (especially its effects in formerly colonized nations) and through migration and immigration.

Psychologists influenced by postcolonial scholarship have critiqued the widely used acculturation model of "successful" immigration generated by cross-cultural psychologists. In this model, it is assumed that there is a universal process that unfolds for all immigrants (regardless of history, politics, race/ethnicity, gender, etc.) as they encounter their new culture. The process involves invoking one of a number of acculturation strategies. As Bhatia and Ram (2001) have written: "Acculturation strategies refer to the plan or the method that individuals use in responding to stress-inducing new cultural contexts" (p. 40). In the acculturation model, these strategies include (1) assimilation; (2) integration; (3) separation; and (4) marginalization. Assimilation occurs when individuals opt not to maintain their original cultural identity and assume the identity of the new, dominant cultural group by seeking out contact and interactions with this group. Integration occurs when individuals seek to maintain strong ties with both their original ethnocultural group and their new one. Separation is essentially the opposite of assimilation, whereby the traditional cultural identity is maintained by minimizing contact with the new, dominant culture. Finally, marginalization occurs when an individual loses connection with both groups. Research on these processes has largely supported the idea that integration is the most "successful" or optimal strategy in terms of long-term positive outcomes (see Berry, 2019).

In their critique, Bhatia and Ram (2001) note that the acculturation model assumes the universality of psychological processes that unfold without regard to the sociocultural, historical, and political contexts of immigration or to individual differences in race/ethnicities, genders, and so on. These are somehow kept separate from the circuits of dispossession and privilege that are experienced by different immigrant/migrant groups. For example, when integration is posited as the most successful outcome of immigration, how are the power differentials encountered by immigrants navigated? How does one happily integrate identification with a new culture while maintaining connection with the original one? Critical scholars suggest different metaphors that take into account such complexities, such as living in the borders or developing hyphenated selves. Living in the borders is described as being trapped in the in-between. Developing a hyphenated self "involves a constant process of negotiation, intervention, and mediation that are connected to a larger set of political and historical practices that are in turn linked to and shaped by issues of race, gender, sexuality and power" (Bhatia & Ram, 2001, p. 14).

Also problematic is the assumption, in the acculturation model, that there is a clear and bounded differentiation between the traditional home culture and the new host culture, and that these two cultures are themselves static, homogenous, and self-contained. Hermans and Kempen (1998) contend that globalization has seriously destabilized any such assumptions. As they have written, "In an increasingly interconnected world society, the conception of independent, coherent, and stable cultures becomes increasingly irrelevant" (Hermans & Kempen, 1998, p. 1111).

Hermans and Kempen apply their critique to the common practice in cross-cultural psychology of identifying and reifying cultural dichotomies, such as individualism versus collectivism or home country versus host country, which also tend to conflate culture with geography and, specifically, nation-states. This, as they and others point out, effaces the considerable cultural heterogeneity and hybridity within countries (especially formerly colonized countries) and cannot account for the ongoing, dynamic interchange of knowledge, culture, and contact among countries. They propose, instead, the study of cultural contact zones – the places where different cultures mix and meet.

Other scholars have highlighted how the experiences of diasporic communities and transnational migrants challenge a homogenous conceptualization of culture and a simplified cultural dichotomies approach. This approach cannot adequately capture the continuous back and forth negotiations between/among cultural spaces experienced by these groups. As Bhatia (2008) states:

> We know that concepts such as race, class, and power are intricately woven with the fabric of culture and their meanings are recreated in the diasporic spaces. However, both cross-cultural and cultural psychology have yet to take up the mantle of exploring how the concepts that make up the components of culture acquire new meanings within the contexts of transnational migration. (p. 315)

Further, Bhatia reminds us that the modern nation-state continues to operate under and enforce colonial and imperialist policies, and that differential flows of migration from Third-World postcolonial societies to First-World societies cast serious doubt on the idea that culture can be "circumscribed and defined by national boundaries" (p. 317). Psychological studies based on the reification of national "cultures" (Japanese, Indian, American, Mexican, Brazilian, etc.) are thus, at best, incomplete.

3 Gender in Cross-Cultural and Cultural Psychology

Having now mapped out – albeit selectively – the conceptual development of gender in psychology and the broad contours of the cross-cultural and cultural psychology approaches, in Section 3 I examine how gender has been taken up in each of these two approaches. That is, how does gender figure into the body of work undertaken by cross-cultural psychologists? How does gender figure into cultural psychology? After outlining some high-level features of these relationships, I will give a couple of examples of how gender has been included in cross-cultural studies and in studies conducted from a cultural psychology perspective.

3.1 Cross-Cultural Psychology: Gender Differences across Cultures

Just as cross-cultural psychologists tend to view culture as a relatively static variable that is isomorphic with nation, so too is gender largely viewed as a static variable that is isomorphic with sex category. Notwithstanding that cross-cultural psychology largely uses binary gender as the variable of interest, it also does so in a way that presumes that the meaning of (even binary) gender is relatively fixed and universal. It does not interrogate how culture makes up gender and vice versa. In this way, cross-cultural psychology is a close cousin, conceptually, to work on gender or sex differences in psychology. In fact, in many cases, it combines the two, asking "Does the same gender difference hold true across different cultural (read 'national') contexts?"

Sieben (2016) undertook a review of all studies published in the *Journal of Cross Cultural Psychology* (*JCCP*) from its inception in 1970 that had sex, gender, femininity, or masculinity in the title. This resulted in seventy-seven articles. Forty-one of these seventy-seven articles reported on gender differences across cultures. That is, both gender and culture were treated as variables, typically in a 2X2 design, where men and women in two different national contexts were compared. Most studies found significant gender differences in both contexts and used quantitative methods.

The remaining thirty-six articles were fairly evenly distributed among the following categories: studies of gender roles in different countries (e.g., administering sex role inventories developed in the United States in different populations); comparing the content of gender stereotypes or knowledge about stereotypes across cultures; comparison of gender-related values and attitudes in different cultures; studies of gender socialization; administration of quantitative measures of femininity and masculinity as a cultural dimension; or testing a scale of femininity in a different context.

Sieben summarizes by stating that cross-cultural psychology tends to treat gender, like culture, as an independent variable; compares gender differences across cultures (often defined as countries) as a means of establishing their universal nature; uses mainly quantitative methods; and draws on mainstream social-psychological concepts such as stereotypes, attitudes, values, sex roles, and gender socialization. These conclusions are supported by other content analyses of this journal (see Best & Everett, 2010; Cretchley, Rooney, & Gallois, 2010).

As one illustrative example of the way gender is typically treated in these types of studies, Sieben (2016) summarizes a study of sex differences in visual-spatial performance among Ghanaian and Norwegian adults (Amponsah & Krekling, 1997). In this study, four tests of spatial ability were administered to university students in each country to determine whether sex differences existed, and their structure and size. The authors' results indicated that men outscored women on three of the four tests in each country. The size and structure of the differences were the same across countries. Although possible explanations for these differences are discussed, the authors cannot (and do not) offer any definitive statements. Sieben notes that in the large majority of *JCCP* articles on gender differences, cultural-level explanations are offered (rather than biological explanations), though the studies, by design, can only remain descriptive. In a small handful, evolutionary theory is used to explain the differences. The exact role of culture in this particular study remains unclear, and no explanation for the comparison of Ghana and Norway is given other than, perhaps, to show how two supposedly very different cultures show similarities, thus lending support to the idea that this gender difference is universal. As she points out, however, university students may be more similar than different from each other across countries than other members of each population, thus mitigating the assumed dissimilarity of the two countries/cultures.

As Sieben's survey reveals, very few articles in this journal of cross-cultural psychology offer insight into the ways that culture structures gender and gender structures culture. Culture remains isomorphic with nationality; gender is untheorized; and gender differences are described but not explained.

3.2 Cultural Psychology: Exploring Gender

Cultural psychology approaches gender quite differently than cross-cultural psychology, albeit with some variability in theoretical approaches (for examples, see the chapters in Kirschner & Martin, 2010). Alongside her review of the *Journal of Cross-Cultural Psychology*, Sieben (2016) also conducted a search for gender, sex, femininity, and masculinity in the journal *Cultural Psychology*, which began publication in 1995. She found twenty articles that included sex, gender, femininity, and/or masculinity in the title or keywords (note that because it began publication much later than *JCCP* and publishes fewer issues per year, quantitative comparisons are not meaningful). In several of these, gender was tangential to the main focus. In about half of the remaining articles, women's identities, narratives, and roles were explored. In the rest, the focus was on masculinity.

She concludes from her search that questions of gender identity and how gender is narrated tend to predominate in this journal. Gender is presumed to be a culturally laden category, not a static variable, and the goal is to understand and explore the relationship between gender and culture; how culture constitutes gender; or how gender is embedded in culture. Methods tend to be qualitative, including narrative and discursive approaches, and gender itself – not gender differences – is the focus of inquiry.

Sieben notes that in many of these studies there was deep and rich description, but little by way of explanation. That is, although cross-cultural psychology does not offer explanations for gender differences, cultural psychology also rarely advances our understanding of *why* gender is narrated and enacted in certain ways and not others.

As one example of a typical article in this journal, Sieben describes an ethnographic study of women working in an Islamic women-only bank in Dubai. The researcher's orienting question is "How do female Islamic finance practitioners negotiate gender identity formation within the context of modern globalizing processes?" (Ahmed, 2012, p. 543). The author concludes that women-only banks allow for the coexistence of modern and traditional identities without violating Shari'a law. Although the article is rich in description, Sieben (2016) notes that there is little attention paid to the actual psychological processes through which these women's dual identities are formed; most attention is paid to the cultural norms and values at play in this particular setting. Interestingly, this may be a rather persistent problem for cultural psychologists: How, exactly, does culture infiltrate subjectivity? What is the best way to think about this relationship, and this process?

Magnusson & Marecek (2012) point out that many theorists in cultural psychology assume that identities are constructed through narrative. An individual's identity narratives always draw on the multiple cultural narratives that are available, including new ones that become available through transnational migration. Other scholars combine narrative approaches with the use of theoretical frameworks such as the dialogical self to explore how people living in and between different cultures, including transnational migrants and members of diasporic communities, narrate their identities (see Bhatia, 2002).

As one example of a dialogical approach that engages with gender, Bhatia and Ram (2004) explore how South Asian women living in transnational diasporic communities negotiate their multiple, and at times conflicting, identities by analysing the multiple voices of the hybrid self. They position their study as an alternative to mainstream studies that examine the immigration process through the lens of a universal, linear acculturation model. The experience of living in transnational diaspora, they argue, profoundly challenges this model. Diasporic communities are defined as those that identify and act as a collective community in forging and maintaining links, including social relations, between their cultures of origin and settlement. Examples include Iranian-Canadians, Black-British, and Asian-Indians. Bhatia & Ram (2004) suggest that alternative models are necessary for understanding these experiences. As they put it, "we employ a dialogical approach to understand the formation of hybridized identities and hyphenated selves of the second-generation South Asian-American women. Adopting a dialogical approach that focuses on the multiplicity of subject positions allows us to highlight the multiple, alternating, and often paradoxical "voices" of the hybrid self" (Bhatia & Ram, 2004, p. 226).

In a dialogical framework, emphasis is placed on the multivocality expressed through different – alternating and shifting – subject positions, which are themselves dependent on the sociocultural setting. That is, some settings will privilege some voices over others. In one of their case studies, Bhatia and Ram focus on the dialogical process of polyphonization to demonstrate how we might conceptualize this hybrid or hyphenated self. In polyphonization, there is opposition among voices and subvoices that knit together to form a loosely differentiated self-structure. They draw on an intergenerational dialogue between second-generation South Asian-Indian-American Sayantini DasGupta and her mother, which describes how, growing up in an all-White midwestern US suburb, she was immersed in an ocean of blonde hair and blue eyes. These characteristics defined the standard beauty ideal for women, which she could never attain. She was also on the receiving end of racial slurs and lacked any role models for her developing sexual self-concept.

Although DasGupta painfully internalized these external voices of othering, they were not the only voices. Coexisting with these denigrating voices based on culturally contingent gender and racial norms were the voices emanating from the Western construction of South Asian women as exotic and mysterious. DasGupta described this as being caught in a dual metaphor of asexual (ugly, racialized, intellectual) and hypersexual (Kama Sutra). Layered on top of this, DasGupta experienced the within-group norms around the desirability of fairer skin, coupled with the strong expectation that she would marry within her own cultural group. Second-generation women are expected to abide by the expectations, customs, and rituals surrounding sexuality and marriage in the homeland, even as they encounter and negotiate very different norms and practices in their land of settlement.

One of these originary cultural expectations is that the Indian woman will be sexually chaste and demure. As Bhatia and Ram (2004) sum up: "So while the South Asian-American woman is imbued with the contradictory voices of being simultaneously 'ugly' and 'exotic' in relation to the larger mainstream White culture, she is also permeated with notions of beauty and chastity specified by her own community" (p. 231). They emphasize that in direct contestation of traditional acculturation models that see the harmonious integration of the dominant values of the homeland and land of settlement as the optimal endpoint of successful immigration, members of transnational diasporic communities do not experience this integration. Rather, using the concept of voice allows a much more complex, shifting, at times contradictory, and dynamic experience of self to emerge. There is a constant process of negotiation and contestation among different voices that is at times painful, never finished, and certainly not captured by the notion of integration. Moreover, the voices share an asymmetrical relationship with each other both within the original cultural group and between this group and the culture(s) of settlement, stratified by considerations of gender, race, and nationality.

As another example of the use of narrative methods in understanding the gendered effects of migration, feminist psychologist Oliva Espín has conducted interviews to gather the life narratives of a diverse group of women immigrants to the United States, focusing specifically on how migration affected their experiences of gender roles and sexuality (Espín, 1999; Espín, 2006). Espín, who has spent her career conducting psychotherapy with immigrant women, contends that for migrant women, more so than for men, the act of crossing boundaries yields opportunities for redefining and transforming sexuality and gender roles, but that this process is rarely linear and straightforward. It involves both losses and gains. For many immigrant communities facing multiple uncontrollable changes and stressors, policing and enforcing "traditional" gender roles in the private world of the home becomes one way of exerting control and maintaining connection with the culture of origin. Indeed, she finds that some immigrant women actively participate in adhering to these traditions even when they appear to curtail their new freedoms and opportunities for self-fulfillment. In addition, Espín finds that language, namely the need to learn a second language due to immigration, plays a powerful and revealing role in how these women narrate their sexual experiences. For some, learning the English language was coincident with their adolescent sexual development or with coming out as a lesbian; thus, they preferred to talk about sexuality in English, their second language. Less frequently, some women found their first language to be more expressive and arousing the language of emotions, and could not imagine "making love in English" (Espín, 2006, p. 249). Overall,

Espín concludes that access to more than one language expands – pushes at the boundaries of – what is "knowable" or "tellable" for immigrant women.

4 Culture in the US Psychology of Women and Gender

In Section 3 I examined how gender has been positioned in the fields of cross-cultural and cultural psychology. One might expect, given the centrality of gender to personal, social, cultural, political, and economic organization, that it should be a central analytic focus in both of these fields. In cultural psychology especially, the sociocultural constitution of gender should be foundational. Despite the selected examples discussed earlier, a quick and admittedly unsystematic assessment suggests that it is not. For example, of the fifty-two chapters in the first edition of the *The Handbook of Culture and Psychology*, only one chapter is explicitly oriented around gender (Madureira, 2012). In the second edition, comprised of twenty-three chapters, there remains only one chapter on the topic (Best & Puzio, 2019). In the second edition of *Cross-Cultural Psychology: Contemporary Themes and Perspectives* (Keith, 2019), there is, laudably, a section on gender and sex roles. However, this section is comprised of only two chapters out of a total of thirty-four chapters in the entire book (see Lips & Lawson, 2019; Kite, Togans, & Schultz, 2019). Sieben (2016), in her overview of research on gender in four "culture-inclusive" branches of psychology (cultural-historical psychology, critical psychology, action-oriented cultural psychology, and social constructionism), concludes that of the four, only one – namely, Mary and Kenneth Gergen's social constructionist framework (e.g., Gergen, 2011) – makes gender a central analytic concept. That is likely largely attributable to the fact that Mary Gergen was an explicitly feminist psychologist.

A subfield of psychology in which women and gender are central concerns developed around the same time that cross-cultural psychology was becoming institutionalized in the United States in the early 1970s. The emergence of a distinct subfield devoted to the psychological study of women and gender (sometimes also called feminist psychology) was certainly not a uniquely US phenomenon; the institutional trajectories of this (or an equivalent) field in other parts of the world have been, just as they were in the US, shaped by socio-historical, cultural, and political events that unfolded in different ways and at different times, often in tandem with broader-based women's movements. I explore some of these developments in the concluding section of this Element.

In this section, I provide a brief historical overview of the emergence and development of the psychology of women and gender in the United States, and then give specific attention to how scholars and practitioners identified with this field; that is, feminist psychologists who have conceptualized, approached, and studied culture. In the United States, the issue of "culture" is often linked with race/ethnicity, although they are clearly not equivalent or reducible one to the other. Nonetheless, women of color have taken the lead in developing theory and practice that attend not only to gender but also to the intersections of gender with race/ethnicity and other social categories such as class, sexual orientation, religion, and immigration status that are integral to understanding the multicultural composition of the United States.

4.1 Emergence of the Psychology of Women and Gender: A View from the United States

The emergence of a distinct field identified as "psychology of women and gender" took place in the United States in a very specific cultural and political moment. It was catalyzed by the US women's liberation movement of the late 1960s and early 1970s, which itself drew from the model of the US Civil Rights movement that had preceded it. Spurred by a new feminist consciousness, a significant number of women psychologists began to organize and demand multiple changes in their field, and in society. Their demands for change were multifaceted and reverberated well beyond the discipline (Rutherford & Pettit, 2015).

Here I outline some of the institutional reforms that this early feminist challenge set in motion in US psychology. I then describe how feminist psychologists critiqued psychological theory and practice that overwhelmingly centered the White, largely US/European, male experience. In the third section I examine how this critique affected the practices of counseling and therapy as developed by feminist psychologists, many of whom have been/are women of color. Along the way, I outline proposals for new epistemologies and theoretical frameworks for the study of women and gender that incorporate considerations of race/ethnicity, class, and culture (for more extended treatments of the history of the psychology of women and gender in the United States, see Chrisler & McHugh, 2011; Rutherford & Granek, 2010; Rutherford, Marecek, & Sheese, 2012).

4.1.1 Institutional Reforms

In 1969, a group of women met at the American Psychological Association (APA) convention to discuss several concerns. Although APA was the largest organization for psychology in the country (and remains so), there were few female speakers at the convention and no coverage of issues related to or of concern to women. There was no day care offered at the convention, making it difficult for many women to participate. Later, protest would also coalesce around the paucity of women journal editors and reviewers, the lack of women in APA leadership positions and as award recipients, job ads at the on-site Employment Bureau that stipulated "men only," and outright sexual har-assment that ran rampant throughout the institution and the profession. These women formed the Association for Women in Psychology (AWP), and in 1970 a small subgroup pressed the APA leadership to address and rectify these problems (see Tiefer, 1991, for a history of the AWP in this period).

As a result of their pressure, the APA established the task force on the Status of Women in Psychology, which surveyed the APA and recommended a number of reforms including the founding of a division that would focus on the psychology of women. In 1973, Division 35, now the Society for the Psychology of Women, was formed. The same year, the task force itself was commuted to a permanent Committee on Women and Psychology (CWP) that would exist within the APA governance structure. In 1977, a Women's Programs Office was also established, now housed within the Public Interest Directorate (for an examination of these and other institutional changes, see Scarborough & Rutherford, 2018; for a review of the work of the CWP from 1973–2013, see Chrisler et al., 2013)

These bodies have all worked to document and increase the participation and recognition of women in the APA and the broader field. Although women in general have gained significant ground in terms of absolute numbers, it remains clear that when the category "women" is broken down by race/ethnicity, women of color are still not represented in US psychology in proportion to their numbers in the US population. The history of Division 35 itself is illustrative with respect to attempts to bring more racial and ethnic diversity into the field. For its part, AWP has also grappled with these issues, especially in intersection with sexual and gender diversity.

As Russo and Dumont (1997) have noted, diversity and inclusion have been central concerns – not only of feminist psychology – but of the Division specific-ally, since its earliest years. One of the ways Division 35 has worked to ensure more diversity is to create sections devoted to supporting the participation and work of racial/ethnic and sexual minority women. The first of these sections was formally established in 1984: the Section on the Psychology of Black Women (Section I). The roots of the Section go back to 1976, when the task force on Black Women's Concerns was formed. The original priorities of the group were defined as (1) the identification of persons interested in Black women's concerns; (2) the identification of extant research and writing on Black women; (3) research on the Black woman's role as worker; and (4) a compilation of data on demographic variables (Murray, 1977). A proposal to fund the development of a resource bibliography on Afro-American women and psychology was drawn up. In 1977, the task force presented "Psychological Perspectives on Black Women: A Selected Bibliography of Recent Citations," consisting of 140 published articles, dissertations, and books covering the years 1975–1976. This was positively received and with further work eventually grew to more than 1,300 references. In 1982, the Division's journal, *Psychology of Women Quarterly*, published a special issue featuring research on Black women that was guest edited by Saundra Rice Murray and Patricia Bell Scott (Murray & Scott, 1982). As they noted in their introduction, "Our own research experiences reveal that Black women remain invisible persons in American psychology" (p. 259).

The task force members also discussed the importance of maintaining an ongoing presence in the Division. To this end they recommended that the task force become a standing committee with the chair elected by the committee members. Despite some initial hesitation on the part of the Division's executive committee, the Committee on Black Women's Concerns (CBWC) was successfully formed. CBWC subsequently worked with the Women's Program Office at APA to compile and publish a directory of Black women in psychology. In 1984, the committee was replaced by a Section on the Psychology of Black Women, as noted earlier.

Since its inception, the Section has developed an award program, convention programming focusing on the history and concerns of Black women, and the sponsorship of an annual dance at the APA convention, which is used to support important social causes. Perhaps most importantly, the Section provides a place where conversations about the concerns and issues of Black women and Black women psychologists are at the center, not at the margins (hooks, 1984).

A year after the task force on Black Women's Concerns was formed, a task force on the Concerns of Hispanic Women (now Hispanic Women/Latinas) was established. Early initiatives of the task force included convention programming relevant to Hispanic women and compiling a directory of Hispanic women in psychology. The task force became a committee in 1986 and an official section in 2003. In 1962 Dr. Martha Bernal was the first Latina to be awarded a PhD in psychology in the United States. Bernal conducted research on the development of ethnic identity and worked tirelessly to create a pipeline for Latinas in psychology. She developed and promoted clinical training programs attentive to ethnic minority mental health and held many pivotal institutional roles, such as helping to establish the Board of Ethnic Minority Affairs in the American Psychological Association (George, 2012).

In 1983, a task force on Lesbian Issues was formed. Paralleling the institutional development of the task force on Hispanic Women, it became a committee in 1986 and a Section in 2003. It changed its name to the Section on Lesbian, Bisexual, and Transgender Concerns in 2010 to be more inclusive of a range of sexual and gender identities. Like other sections, it coordinates convention programming, an awards program, and a newsletter.

In 1979, a task force on the Concerns of Asian Women was formed. It became a committee in 2005 and a section (Section V) in 2008, whereupon it changed its name to the Section on Asian Pacific American Women's concerns. Finally, although a task force on the Concerns of Native American Women was formed as early as 1984, the small number of women and their geographic distribution made momentum difficult to achieve. However, in 2011, Section VI, Alaska Native/American Indian/Indigenous Women was formed.

The Sections have been important sites for leadership development. Since 1992, the presidents of Division 35 have become increasingly diverse. In 1996, the first openly lesbian president of the Division was elected. Starting in 1991, eight African-American women have served as presidents. To date, there have also been three Latina presidents and two Asian-American presidents. This leadership pipeline extends outside the Division to the higher levels of APA governance, including the APA presidency to which several women-of-color presidents of Division 35 have been elected.

One of the primary activities of each Division president is to appoint and support task forces on areas/subjects that they would like to promote. Presidential task forces generally produce a resource, such as a book, database, or conference, on their topic. Since the 1990s, Division presidents have sponsored task forces on a range of issues, including the future of feminist psychological practice, feminist perspectives on sizeism, and internationalizing the psychology of women curriculum. Several task forces have taken on issues specifically relevant to women and girls of color, such as the task force on Healthy Development of Sexually Diverse Indigenous Girls and Girls of Color, and the task force on South and West Asian Women.

It is clear that, within an organization that focuses on women and gender, supporting racial/ethnic diversity has also been a central concern. This concern has extended to critiques of the research literature in psychology and to its practices and theories. Although in its earliest form the feminist critique of psychology primarily targeted its androcentric bias, in response to the interventions of many women of color it would eventually embrace a more explicitly intersectional framework that highlights the interlocking nature of gender, race/ ethnicity, class, and other social categories in shaping women's – and indeed all peoples' – experience.

4.1.2 Critiques of Androcentric and White/Eurocentric Research

In addition to creating institutional space and material support for psychology of women, early feminists also strove to create a more relevant body of research, to address and reform harmful and exploitative research and professional practices, and to create new ones based on feminist principles. They argued that psychology had an unrelenting androcentric bias, taking the (White) male as the invisible standard against which all others were compared (see Broverman et al., 1970) and conducting research and developing theory solely with men and then generalizing to all people. Carol Gilligan's critique of Kohlberg's moral theory has been an oft-cited example of this kind of critique (see Gilligan, 1982), but Gilligan's work has also been critiqued for essentially repeating this process with White women, namely, that her work generalizes findings on the primacy of an ethic of care from this group to all others. As other scholars have pointed out, gender is but one social category within which such differences need to be situated. Carol Stack, in her narrative research with African American adolescents and adults who were return migrants to the American south, showed that moral reasoning cannot be understood without attending also to class, culture, racial and ethnic formation, and region. In addition to gender, these all "shape the resources within which we construct morality" (Stack, 1994, p. 292).

Feminist psychologists also pointed out that in male-centered psychology, very little psychological research was devoted to topics, issues, or experiences unique to women, except as they were made into problems or pathologies (Crawford & Marecek, 1989). Other feminists charged that the diagnostic systems and nomenclature used by psychologists were infused with androcentric norms about mental health, and many were outright misogynistic (see Caplan, 1985; Dodd, 2015).

To start to rectify this, journals devoted specifically to research on the psychology of women and gender were founded. In the United States, these included *Sex Roles, Psychology of Women Quarterly,* and *Women & Therapy.* Somewhat later, in the 1990s, the journal *Feminism & Psychology* was initiated. This latter journal was started in the United Kingdom, has typically foregrounded qualitative research, and been more intentionally international in terms of its editorial group, authors, and topics. Other trappings of institutionalization in the 1970s included the first psychology of women classes and the first textbooks devoted specifically to the topic (see Unger, 2010). Early on, many of these textbooks gave ample coverage to sex differences research. One even had a section devoted to women in cross-cultural perspective (Hyde & Rosenberg, 1976).

In the early 1970s, feminist psychologists took on the task of critiquing psychology's traditional measurement of masculinity and femininity, a project, they argued, that uncritically and unreflectively drew upon and reinstantiated sex-role stereotypes, and positioned these sets of traits as mutually exclusive (see Constantinople, 1973). To start to address these problems,

Sandra Bem developed the Bem Sex Role Inventory (Bem, 1974), which conceptualized masculinity and femininity as nonorthogonal sets of traits, though it still drew largely on stereotypical notions of male and female sex roles (see Morawski, 1985). Bem proposed that people who endorsed relatively equal numbers of feminine and masculine traits were psychologically androgynous and developed a body of work on gender schema theory (Bem, 1981). Around the same time, Janet Spence also developed a widely used scale called the Personal Attributes Questionnaire that, like Bem's formulation, enabled the independent assessment of both masculinity and femininity (Spence & Helmreich, 1978).

Another area that preoccupied early feminist psychologists, and continues to preoccupy the field, is that of sex or gender differences. In an early attempt to establish the extent, kind, and origins of male-female sex differences, Maccoby and Jacklin undertook a systematic review of the literature and published *The Psychology of Sex Differences* in 1974. Surveying more than 1,400 studies, they found consistent evidence for sex differences in only four out of the eighty areas of behavior they reviewed (Maccoby & Jacklin, 1974). Nonetheless, studying how men and women differ on a whole range of psychological and behavioral traits has preoccupied psychologists, including cross-cultural psychologists, to this day.

This line of research has polarized feminist psychologists in several ways (See Kitzinger, 1994). There are those who argue that women and men are more similar than different, and the constant focus on sex differences obscures this important point (see Hyde, 2005). There are also those who argue that the entire sex differences question is not a feminist question; that "different" is never "equal"; and that women's difference from men will always be taken as a sign of women's inferiority (Rutherford, 2007; Unger, 1979). Gender differences, like race differences, set up "invidious comparisons" (Cole & Stewart, 2001). Additionally, a focus on establishing differences between men and women contributes to an essentializing stance that draws attention away from the processes through which gender, and thus gender differences, are constructed in the first place. The sociocultural construction of gender – through performance and through language – has also been a central research focus for many feminist psychologists and some cultural psychologists (see Gavey, 1989; Gergen, 2001; Kessler & McKenna, 1978). Additionally, gender differences research often uncritically accepts the notion of binary sex and gender, forcing the comparison of males and females despite ample evidence that neither sex nor gender are themselves binary (Hyde et al., 2019). Nonetheless, for many researchers, a focus on sex/gender differences continues to generate product-ive – and often well publicized – programs of research.

Although the earliest feminist critiques of psychology focused almost solely on the lack of attention to women, to gender issues, and to the importance of a consideration of social context and power in generating a meaningful psychology of women (e.g., Weisstein, 1971), feminist psychologists also came to insist on the consideration of race/ethnicity, class, and sexual orientation as central aspects of women's lives that shape their psychological and social experiences. In 1990, Pamela Trotman Reid and Lillian Comas-Díaz edited a special issue of *Sex Roles* on gender and ethnicity. Surveying the state of the psychology of women at the time, they wrote: "When gender studies began to burgeon in the late 1960's and 1970's, an urgent request was made that men not be the standard for behavior. Yet decades later it appears that the standard was only broadened to include White females . . . . [E]thnicity as a status variable has been largely ignored within the context of gender issues" (Reid & Comas-Díaz, 1990, p. 399). They noted too that in the context of psychological studies involving attention to race/ethnicity and culture, the discussion of gender issues was largely absent; further, discussions of racism in psychology often omitted considerations of sexism, and vice versa.

To address this, feminist psychologists, many of whom were women of color, began to investigate the complex relationship of gender to race/ethnicity, class, sexual orientation, religion, immigration status, and other sociocultural categories. They argued that the experience of gender could not be understood fully if separated from the experience of class and race. In this they were echoing the insights of Black feminists in the 1980s who were developing Black feminist theory and critiquing the field of women's studies for being White-centric (see Collins, P. H., 1990; Dill, 1983; hooks, 1981). They were also invoking what Hancock (2016) has termed "intersectionality-like" thinking or what Cooper has termed "proto-intersectionality theorizing" (Cooper, 2016) in the sense that they were invoking the dynamics of intersectionality without naming it as such.

The term "intersectionality" was explicitly introduced by Black feminist legal scholar Kimberle Crenshaw in 1989 in the context of antidiscrimination law that considered race and gender discrimination separately, and race and gender as single axis categories of difference. This, she pointed out using examples from case law, occluded the rights and experiences of those in the intersections, namely, Black women (Crenshaw, 1989). Although not using the term "intersectionality" itself, feminist psychologists of color were, at this same time, insisting that the experiences of women of color could not be adequately studied or theorized if gender and the experience of sexism were assumed to be of sole and primary importance. They pointed out that race/ethnicity and racism often preceded gender and sexism for women of color, but moreover, gender, race, and class needed to be considered simultaneously to fully capture the complexity of women's experiences.

In 1991, Lillian Comas-Díaz presented a historical outline of the "dynamic interplay" between feminism and ethnicism, defined as the movement to promote social, economic, and political equality among ethnic and racial groups. As she put it, ethnicism "stresses the pervasive interaction of ethnicity, culture, race, gender, discrimination, and oppression in the lives of people of color" (Comas-Díaz, 1991, p. 598). As she demonstrated, the goals and priorities of feminism and ethnicism have often been in tension. Women-of-color feminists, unlike White feminists, may not, and often do not, experience sexism as their primary oppression. Comas-Díaz then outlined five feminist principles that were particularly applicable to women of diverse ethnicities.

The first, relevance of women's contexts, emphasized the central importance of sociocultural context in theorizing and understanding diverse women's lives, in contrast to purely intrapsychic approaches. Though this feminist critique of mainstream (psychodynamic and trait-based personality) psychology had been made earlier, Comas-Díaz highlighted the substantial influence of race-based political and economic factors on diverse women's experiences. The second principle, that differences are not deficiencies, drew attention to the impact of cultural factors on differences among groups, leading to unique needs and circumstances that are not pathologies, just differences. The third, equalization of power, called attention to the right of every person to share equally in the power in any given situation and pointed out that women of color are often doubly oppressed by gender and race. The fourth, empowerment, acknowledged that to share equally in power, women of color must recognize the negative effects of racism, sexism, and classism on their lives, use tools to overcome these effects, and perceive themselves as agents in developing solutions to these problems. This includes identifying the social forces that impinge on their well-being. The fifth, social action, returns attention to the social and structural origins of the oppression of women of color and the need, therefore, for social change as a means of eliminating this oppression.

In another early critique of the failure of psychological research to differentiate the experiences of women on the basis of race/ethnicity and class, Reid (1993) pointed out the lack of research on poor women, whom she described as "shut up and shut out" of psychological research. But Reid's indictment went much further than simply pointing out that psychologists had yet to take up class and classism as objects of psychological research. Instead, she pointed out that the White middle class was overwhelmingly taken as the standard for all people in terms of being included as research participants, but also in terms of norms, standards, and values. Even in feminist psychology, the White middle-class woman was taken as the standard against which all others were compared. As Reid (1993) noted, "Feminists have worked insistently to overturn the use of the male norm. Unfortunately, the acceptance of both race and class standards has remained virtually untouched. As White middle-class men were treated as the standard for people, White middle-class women are now treated as the standard of appropriate female behavior" (p. 138). This created a psychology that automatically "othered" anyone other than the White middle class that reserved questions about race for people of color (as if being White were not a race) and questions about social class for working class and poor people (ignoring the study of privilege). Reid concluded by calling for a firm commitment from feminist psychologists (and indeed all psychologists) to study women in multiple contexts, but especially in different socioeconomic conditions. She stated that the goal of feminist psychology must be to conduct research that "provides a meaningful analysis of gender as it is experienced in many different contexts" (p. 147).

Building on this pioneering work of feminist psychologists of color, and drawing a direct line to this work and back to Crenshaw and her Black feminist predecessors (e.g., Combahee River Collective, 1978), intersectionality was explicitly articulated in US feminist psychology as a conceptual/analytic tool for both research and practice in the early 2000s. In 2006, Isis Settles published a study of Black women's identities that used both quantitative and qualitative methods to show the inseparability of racial and gender identities for Black women using intersectionality as a framework (Settles, 2006). In 2008, a special issue of the journal *Sex Roles* focused on intersectionality (see Shields, 2008). In this issue, Lisa Bowleg used her program of research on Black lesbian experience to explore the methodological challenges, for psychologists, of viewing multiple social identities, not as additive, but as mutually constitutive (Bowleg, 2008). Valerie Purdie-Vaughns and Richard Eibach proposed a model to explain how ideologies of androcentrism, ethnocentrism, and heterocentrism operate to make people who have multiple subordinated-group identities come to be seen as nonprototypical members of any one subordinated group, and are thus rendered "intersectionally invisible" (Purdie-Vaughns & Eibach, 2008). Elizabeth Cole (2008) provided a conceptual exploration of intersectionality to urge psychologists to move away from a "categorical" approach, in which intersectionality connotes the study of individuals who belong to particular multidimensional social categories, toward "political intersectionality," a concept outlined by Crenshaw that considers how social categories come into being "through practices of individuals, institutions and cultures rather than primarily as characteristics of individuals" (p. 445). This, Cole argues, can form the basis for a coalitional politics that transcends the limits of the identity politics and oppression Olympics (Hancock, 2011) that the focus on multiple subordinated identities sometimes sets up.

In political intersectionality, the focus is on how political institutions such as organizations, social movements, and public policies misrepresent or ignore the concerns and agendas of those with multiple marginalized social identities. For example, how do workplace harassment policies based on the experiences of White women with sexual harassment and Black men with racial discrimination fail to address the experiences of Black women (see Buchanan & Ormerod, 2002)? Or, how have social movements such as the Women's Health Movement occluded the concerns of sexual minority, low-income, and/or racialized women, especially when it comes to reproductive health? How is a focus on reproductive justice an antidote to this occlusion (Ross, 2017)?

The shift in focus from identity categories to the organizations, structures, and policies that make them meaningful makes political intersectionality a more challenging approach for psychologists trained in an individualist ontology, but, as Cole shows, it is a potentially fruitful source of insights to generate effective coalitional activism. Using interviews with activists conducted for the Global Feminisms Project based at the University of Michigan, Cole (2008) gives several examples of how political intersectionality was used by activists to identify common political goals that transcended categorical differences among members within social movements. The result was that these differences could be respected and maintained without becoming the basis for unproductive identity politics. Further, the focus on accomplishing a shared political goal could be maintained.

This concern with retaining and nurturing the activist, social justice origins of intersectionality has most recently been taken up by feminist psychologists who worry that its appropriation into psychology has blunted its critical edge and capacity for informing critical praxis (Buchanan, Rios, & Case, 2020; Grzanka, 2020). As Grzanka (2020) has noted, "Intersectionality's popularity also presents opportunities for its dilution and political neutralization, a concern long advanced by Black feminists and other women of color scholars who have witnessed intersectionality's white-washing, cooptation, and appropriation in other disciplines" (p. 244). These scholars advance a renewed focus on the use of intersectionality as a tool for connecting scholarship with activism, for exploring privilege as well as oppression, and for amplifying considerations of structure and power in psychological theory and practice.

Although intersectionality is undeniably one of the most influential conceptual innovations in US feminist psychology over its short history, it has not escaped the criticisms of scholars who claim that it has its own limitations given the ethnocentric context in which it was developed (Grabe & Else-Quest, 2012; Kurtiş & Adams, 2015, 2017; Patil, 2013; Warner, Kurtiş, & Adya, 2020). Transnational feminists highlight how intersectionality has been based on – and largely applied to – the experiences of women in the Global North and is thus insufficiently attentive to the dynamics of coloniality and uneven flows of global power. They argue that the unique experiences of Majority-World (aka "developing world") women that could inform global social justice efforts in a truly transnational sense are not taken into account in intersectional theorizing. Instead, this theorizing has tended, because of its own intellectual and political origins, to reproduce rather than challenge Euro-American domination and contribute to the othering of Majority-World women. This othering often takes the form of portraying these women as helpless, uninformed, and passive victims of their oppressive cultural traditions (Kurtiş & Adams, 2015). By contrast, decolonial intersectionality asks "What can scholars in Western settings learn from the experiences of Majority-World women? How can analyses based on their experiences reveal intersections of oppression – and privilege – that are currently invisible to those in 'the west'? How can it introduce alternatives to the 'neoliberal individualist ontology' that undergirds both US psychology and, historically, US liberal feminism (Kurtiş & Adams, 2017, p. 55)?"

As one example, Kurtiş (2010) has critiqued the Silencing the Self theory of depression, which was developed in the US context (Jack, 1991). Silencing the Self theory proposes that a key component of women's depression is the silencing of their personal desires and needs in response to the gendered burden of care and self-sacrifice characteristic of a patriarchal society. In this view, self-disclosure and self-expression are taken to be paths to intimacy and relational and mental well-being, and their suppression harms women. By questioning the universality of the link between self-expression and mental health, as well as the individualist ontology that is assumed by the theory, Kurtiş revealed how women in the Turkish context used silence in very different ways. Rather than as an act of inhibition that curtailed mental health, some women used silence as a form of self-care, for example. For women in interdependent cultural contexts, silence, Kurtiş pointed out, can be a self-protective act. Additionally, in contexts where the self is constructed as inherently interdependent and relational – not only connected to other humans, but also to the land and to spirituality – silence performs very different functions.

4.1.3 Culture in US Feminist Therapy and Counseling

In addition to critiquing psychological research, feminist psychologists in the 1970s also critiqued practices occurring within the psychotherapeutic context. One of the earliest accomplishments of feminist psychologists was to reveal the power abuses (including sexual exploitation) enacted in the therapy setting, which was at the time dominated by White male therapists (see Chesler, 1972).

Feminist psychologists were instrumental in documenting the sex bias and sex role stereotyping that permeated clinical training and practice, and in demanding that the use of sexual contact in therapy be explicitly prohibited in psychology's ethics code (Kim & Rutherford, 2015). In addition to critiquing extant practices, feminists also began to develop new approaches to therapy that were explicitly feminist. Feminist therapy, in general, attempts to reduce power imbalances between therapist and client, and attend centrally to the social, political, and economic conditions that impinge negatively on women's lives. The focus moves away from resolving internal or intrapsychic "pathologies" toward understanding psychological distress as a legitimate reaction to unjust and exploitative relationship, family, and social systems.

At its inception, feminist therapy – like feminist research – centered the experiences, contexts, and values of White, middle-class women as stand-ins for "all women." As Brown (1995) noted, "Prior to the mid-1980s, there had been little in the literature about feminist therapy theory that directly addressed itself to, or was primarily written by, women who were from outside the dominant White and middle class stratum of society" (p. 145). She noted that the failure of feminist therapy theorists to incorporate the diversity and complexity of the lives of diverse women stemmed, at least in part, from their training in traditional theories of personality and psychopathology. This training, she noted, was itself highly culture-bound (i.e., Eurocentric). Although many White feminist therapists had begun to discern and root out the masculinist, heterocentric, and homophobic biases of therapeutic theory and practice, Brown noted that concomitant racism and classism had been less visible to practitioners who themselves benefited from the privileges of race and class. She noted that assumptions about goals and priorities in feminist therapy frequently reflected highly culture- and class-bound norms that ignored structural and contextual differences among women.

This deficiency in feminist therapy began to be addressed in the 1980s. Feminist therapists, many of whom were women of color, quickly turned their attention to the issue of culture in therapy and the role of culture in mental health. In some cases, this work took the form of outlining the sociocultural issues involved in working with women clients from different racial, ethnic, and cultural groups, such as doing feminist therapy and counseling with mainland Puerto Rican women (Comas-Díaz, 1987), with Black and Hispanic women (Amaro & Russo, 1987; Mays & Comas-Díaz, 1988), and with Latina immigrant women (Espín, 1987). This body of research has built toward a multicultural feminist therapy theory and practice that is explicitly antiracist and based on the experiences of culturally, racially, and sexually diverse women.

Within the mental health professions writ large, this important work has highlighted the need for all therapists to develop awareness of the sociocultural factors affecting their clients' lives and psychological well-being, especially as these may differ from those of the therapist and the largely White-dominated Eurocentric mental health profession itself. In the United States, this awareness has taken the form, especially in the clinical training arena, of developing "cultural competency." Originally, this was a response to the largely culturally insensitive and therefore incompetent body of theory and practice that guided clinical training and was therefore a much-needed antidote to this deficiency. However, as it has evolved in psychology (and other health professions), cultural competency has become a form of recipe knowledge in which practitioners learn a set of facts about different cultural groups and use this set of facts (which conform largely to cultural stereotypes) to alter or supplement "standard" clinical practice. Once the set of facts has been learned, and appropriate steps are taken, the learning process is deemed complete, and cultural competency is seen to have been achieved.

As many cultural psychologists and psychiatrists have pointed out, this was not the original aim of cultural competency as a training paradigm. In this form, cultural competency functions simply to reinforce stereotypes rather than promote active learning and listening on the part of the clinician (see Kirmayer, 2012; Kleinman & Benson, 2006). And although alternative models, such as cultural safety (Smye, Josewski, & Kendall, 2010) – which demands that histories of colonial oppression and violence in the mental health professions are taken into account – and structural competency (Metzl & Hansen, 2014)– which reroutes attention away from individual differences to the structures that differentially affect cultural and ethnoracial groups, have been proposed as alternatives, feminist psychologists have suggested another possibility: intersectional cultural humility (Buchanan, Rios, & Case, 2020).

Intersectional cultural humility requires that therapists be constantly open and attentive to how a client's subjective experience is shaped by multiple aspects of their social context, such as race, gender, and class, which are themselves rooted in particular political, historical, and physical/geographic locations. Intersectional cultural humility is a dynamic and ongoing process, rather than an accomplishment, or a body of knowledge to be mastered. Importantly, it requires ongoing reflection by the therapist on the ways their own privilege, marked by their own intersectional locations, may inhibit their ability to identify and talk about systems of oppression. It requires constant attention to the play of power within the therapy setting and a willingness to learn from and learn with one's clients. It also acknowledges that clients' subjective experiences are themselves dynamic and shifting, and that even within particular cultural and ethnoracial groups, people occupy different inter-sectional locations that acquire different meanings and significance over time (Buchanan, Rios, & Case, 2020). Related to intellectual humility, defined as recognizing and being responsive to the limits of one's knowledge (e.g., Porter & Schumann, 2017; Whitcomb et al., 2017), and – even more deeply – epistemic humility, in which one acknowledges and is responsive to the limits of one's ability to know, intersectional cultural humility thus serves to avoid some of the pitfalls of the cultural competency approach and introduce an explicitly intersectional lens.

5 Culture, History, and Feminist Psychology

To conclude this Element, I move from a consideration of how attention to culture has infused the development of the psychology of women and gender in the United States to a consideration of how the psychology of women and gender itself has developed in relation to its cultural contexts in other parts of the world. As I have shown, attention to culture by feminist psychologists who study gender in the United States has taken different forms but has invariably been influenced by the salient cultural and ethnoracial categories of US history that have been and are used to structure – and regulate – the US population. People occupying these categories are differentially privileged, reflecting the legacies of slavery, internal colonialism, and immigration policies that have produced the intransigent circuits of dispossession and privilege characteristic of US society (Fine & Ruglis, 2009; Weis & Fine, 2012).

An assumption informing this Element is that psychology as a discipline and body of knowledge is itself always embedded in, constituted by, and in turn constitutive of the culture(s) in which it develops. Feminist psychologies are no exception. Given that the study of gender and its relation to other social categories is central to feminist psychology, examining how (and whether) feminist psychologies have developed in different cultural and geopolitical contexts (notwithstanding the complex effects of migration and transnational diaspora, as discussed previously) can reveal much about how gender and gender relations have also developed.

This was, in fact, the orienting assumption and theme of a volume I coedited with colleagues in the United Kingdom, South Africa, and India called *Handbook of International Feminisms: Perspectives on Psychology, Women, Culture, and Rights* (Rutherford, Capdevila, Undurti, & Palmary, 2011). In this volume, we invited self-identified feminist psychologists working in different parts of the world to describe and analyze the interrelationships among psychology, gender, culture, politics, and feminism, both within the academy and beyond, in their national context or geopolitical region. Authors analyzed not only how gender was taken up in psychological theory, research, and practice (and in turn, how psychology influenced gender) but also how gender intersected with class, caste, "race," ethnicity, sexuality, religion, and – in several cases – colonialism. Many authors took a historical perspective on these issues, acknowledging that the emergence, and even existence, of a critical psychology that focuses on gender issues was dependent on sociohistorical and sociopolitical forces and, indeed, in many parts of the world, is nonexistent, precarious, and/or in flux.

In this final section I provide brief overviews of the development and selective contours of feminist psychologies in Brazil, India, and China, highlighting regions outside the Global North to provide a counterweight to the heavily US-based content of most of this Element. Astute readers may note that in making these selections, I have elided "culture" with national context, a practice that some cultural psychologists have critiqued. Indeed, we were aware of this problematic elision when we conceptualized the volume. To try to mitigate this, authors were encouraged to avoid reifying and homogenizing culture and to view political borders as themselves porous, though meaningful, placeholders for their analyses. Indeed, many authors noted the interweaving of developments in their own locales with those in/from other places, demonstrating the – often uneven – flows of intellectual influence, especially between former colonies and their former colonizers, and between the Global North and Global South.

We were also aware that "feminism" and "feminist psychology" themselves are culturally – and politically – saturated terms that are not always used – and may be scrupulously avoided – to characterize the concern with the connection between gender issues and social justice that we were seeking to reconstruct. Thus, "feminist psychology" itself was often flagged by authors in terms of its (problematic) association with Western forms of autonomy, freedom of choice, and equal rights discourse, which interacted in complex ways with extant tensions between tradition and modernity in many societies. Finally, in order to understand the form that any kind of "feminist psychology" might take, it was necessary to place it alongside the histories, status, and forms that psychology (as an academic discipline) itself took in these regions.

5.1 Feminist Psychology as Critical Social Psychology: A View from Brazil

As Nuernberg et al. (2011) note, "Feminist Psychology as a recognized, institutionalized area of research and practice does not exist in Brazil" (p. 109). In their exploration of the status of gender and feminist approaches in Brazilian Psychology (with capital "P" Psychology referring to the institutionalized discipline), the authors note that although the field of gender studies did coalesce in Brazil in tandem with the women's movement of the 1970s, gender studies had a limited impact on psychology, and psychology participated only marginally – compared to other social sciences – in gender studies. Psychology itself as an institutionalized, academic field was in its relative infancy in the 1970s, with the first postsecondary degree programs established in Brazilian universities in the late 1950s and early 1960s.

Gender concerns have primarily entered psychology through social psychology, a subfield of Brazilian Psychology that has been more attuned to social movements and is generally characterized by a critical-historical approach rather than a positivist one (Hutz, Gauer, & Gomes, 2012). Outside of the academy, there have been popularizers of feminism who were psychologists. Nuerenberg et al. (2011) note the writings of Carmen da Silva in the 1970s and early 1980s, a psychologist who wrote frequent articles for a prominent women's magazine on topics deemed "ahead of their time" such as marital and love relations, female sexuality, and women's professional achievements.

In terms of the relationship between the Brazilian women's movement and gender studies, the topics/trends in the former influenced the latter. Specifically, one arm of the women's movement focused on public and political action, targeting issues related to work, legal reforms, health (especially sexual and reproductive health), gender discrimination, and violence against women. Another arm focused on women's subjectivity and interpersonal relations as legitimate sites for feminist reform (i.e., the personal as political). There was a relatively tight relationship between activists and academics, both in terms of issues addressed and participation in the movement (with many feminist academics also participating in activism), although this relationship was not without tension. Some historians of Brazilian gender studies have argued that the relationships among feminist movements, scientific organizations, and university departments have been less conflictual in Brazil than elsewhere. Universities were considered important sites for raising awareness of the conditions affecting women, and consciousness-raising groups were often formed within universities.

Psychology has often been represented as a "feminine" discipline in Brazil, in part because training in psychology encompasses psychosocial care, which is considered feminine and attracts more women. That has not necessarily translated into psychology as a feminist discipline, however, in part because of an insistence on a version of the scientific method that sees gender as an "ideological" and, therefore, not properly scientific concept.

Nonetheless, feminist concerns have entered the discipline through a critical social psychology that emerged most strongly in the 1970s. Although there was a positivist-oriented social psychology in Brazil before this time, its main theoretical influences came from elsewhere (Lewinian field theory; North American scholars), and it was largely comprised of studies of human relations, group dynamics, and national character. In the 1970s, a critical social psychology influenced strongly by historical materialism (an important influence on Latin American psychology more generally) and interdisciplinary in its orientation, began – in part as a response to the reductionist framework embraced by previous scholars. In 1980, an organization devoted to this critical social psychology was established: the Associacao Brasileirade Psicologia Social (ABRAPSO). ABRAPSO became an important organizational arena where groups of female psychologists from the federal universities of Sao Paolo, Minas Gerais, and Rio de Janeiro began to introduce and incorporate gender and feminist issues. ABRASPO has sponsored books in this area, focusing on thematic areas such as violence, abortion, and work, as well as feminist epistemology. It publishes a journal, *Psychology and Society*, that foregrounds research that has social and political relevance. Nonetheless, as Nuernberg et al. (2011) observe, outside of this subfield, psychology in Brazil as a whole continues to devalue gender analysis and feminist contributions.

5.2 Human First, Then Women: A View from China

In their overview of feminist psychology in China, Chen & Cheung (2011) point out that the terms "feminist" and "feminism" are importations of Western vocabulary. Most Chinese women's studies scholars, writers, and artists would not, they note, call themselves feminists. In addition to the negative connotations of the term (which is imbued with Western ideological baggage), a bourgeois preoccupation with gender as opposed to class struggle is considered inimical to the Marxist orientation that characterizes Chinese society and government. In Marxism, gender is subordinate to class. Thus, although the formation of the People's Republic of China in 1949 brought with it almost immediate and comprehensive legal reforms equalizing women's status, many women see their liberation as being tied to nationalistic and socialistic revolution in solidarity with men, not by working against them (as Western feminism is perceived to promote).

Nonetheless, despite a "human first, then women" orientation, there were many scholars in the latter half of the twentieth century, specifically in the 1980s and 1990s, who studied Western feminist theories and practices to understand and improve the lives of Chinese women. They also developed indigenous approaches to promote women's progress and work toward gender equality. Chen & Cheung (2011) describe the development of academic feminism in contemporary China as evolving in three stages.

The first, the "embryonic" stage, during the 1980s, focused on gathering and producing literature about women's issues and largely unfolded within the fields of literature and history. The second, during the 1990s, saw the Year of Women in China (1995) and the convening of the United Nations Fourth World Conference on Women in Beijing. Both of these ignited enthusiasm and interest in feminist studies, especially in the academy. "Feminist" scholarship blossomed, including a monumental work edited by women's studies scholar Li Xiaojiang, *Gender and China*. This brought together works by scholars in women's studies, China studies, history, and cultural studies to analyze women's concerns in China.

What Chen & Cheung (2011) characterize as the third developmental stage of Chinese feminism occurred around the turn of the twenty-first century. This stage was marked by more multidisciplinary engagements with gender (including psychological ones) and a focus on more pragmatic issues. These have included domestic violence and rape, women's employment, sex and reproduction, and women's legal and economic status. It is in this third stage that they discuss some of the major research topics taken up in Chinese "feminist" psychology. Although some of these mirror similar topics taken up by Western scholars (and use similar approaches and techniques), research has also focused on challenges unique to the Chinese context. The problem of "women home alone," for example, and the psychological and social ramifications of China's one-child policy are gender issues unique to women in China.

As Chen & Cheung (2011) point out, there are (theoretically) no class divisions among Chinese women. The major social and economic divide is between rural women and urban women. The experiences of rural women are heavily shaped by a rigid household registration system called *Hukou* in Chinese, which heavily restricts the ability of ordinary Chinese citizens to change their permanent place of residence. With the increasing need for rural farm families to seek supplemental income in cities, especially during the nonfarming season, this has meant that male spouses often migrate to cities to find work, leaving female spouses behind to tend to the household and family. Accordingly, in one study, 80 percent of rural migrant workers were male, and 38 percent of rural adult women were "women home alone" for the majority of the year, if not permanently. This has created significant stresses and psychological problems among many of these women, related to the multiple demands of farming, householding, and caregiving, in the absence of emotional and social support. As a result, the suicide rate of Chinese women is the highest in the world, and most of these are rural women.

Another gender issue unique to women in China is related to the one-child policy, which was introduced in the late 1970s to curb population growth in mainland China (it was modified in the 1980s to allow rural women to have a second child if their first was a girl and to allow ethnic minority women to have additional children). There is a long tradition in China of patrilineal inheritance and preference for sons over daughters. Sons are often ascribed the role of overseeing the care of elderly parents. Even in contemporary China, there is strong cultural resistance to abandoning preference for male offspring, and this has resulted in cases of sex-selective abortion and, in some rural areas, abandonment, even though both are illegal. The Chinese government has intervened with policies to improve old-age security and increase educational levels, but feminist scholars continue to work on how to change well-engrained cultural attitudes and beliefs that impede gender equality and women's quality of life.

Despite these opportunities for a rich, socially relevant feminist psychology in China, Chen & Cheung (2011) note that there has yet to develop a distinct, critically aware form of psychology that has developed its own methods and its own questions. They recommend that one step toward this would be for Chinese feminist psychologists to move outside the restrictive, traditional paradigms and institutions of psychological research, engage more deeply with other disciplines, and embrace interdisciplinarity.

5.3 Women's Issues, the "National Interest," and Globalization: A View from India

In her analysis of the relationships among India's colonial and post-independence history, nationalist discourses, women's movements, religious identities, and the politics of caste, Kumar (2011) notes that the struggle to establish a solid women's movement in India has been complicated by the fact that basic issues of gender justice have often failed to align with the so-called "national interest." As an example, Kumar ties the failure of large-scale collective feminist organizing in India to the perception that feminism requires women to stand outside and in defiance of their religious, political, and cultural surrounds. She notes that other groups, such as right-wing Hindu nationalists, offer opportunities for women to feel empowered without asking them to challenge their religious and cultural beliefs or question patriarchy. In fact, right-wing Hindu women have been given access to cultural and political power precisely because they actively condemn what are construed as "modern/Western" secular, antireligious, and anti-Hindu practices. Thus, Kumar notes, "Despite the violent interpretation of religious identity and its monolithic use for political advantage, the representation of women in right-wing political parties is significantly greater than in the socialist or radical feminist groups" (p. 178).

Additionally, within women's movements themselves, the failure to address caste and class differences has often resulted in the subjugation of Dalit women's and rural and working-class women's rights and needs. According to Kumar (2011), this has resulted in a fragmented movement beset by significant power imbalances, in which upper- and middle-class women struggle to hear and foreground the voices of poor women or speak meaningfully to their experiences. However, one of the legacies of the women's movement as it gained momentum in the 1970s under the influence of a global development agenda that increasingly focused on women was the establishment of the field of women's studies. As Undurti (2007) has noted, women's studies was considered the academic arm of the women's movement. Its focus was on addressing gender inequalities within a critical, emancipatory framework that would combine "theory and activism to influence and remould ideologies that keep women subordinated" (p. 339). Although many social sciences funneled into and were influenced by women's studies, psychology has remained somewhat aloof in its engagement, as it has in many other parts of the world.

As for psychology, although there is a small community of scholars actively working to develop research and practices that are responsive to the unique dynamics of the Indian context (Misra & Gergen, 1993; Sinha, 1986, 1998; for an overview see Kumar, 2006), in large part mainstream psychology in India has been a Western, colonial import that relies on the methods and epistemologies of positivist science. As a result, the focus of feminist psychologists has been on "women's issues" rather than explicitly feminist concerns, and Kumar (2011) rather pessimistically concludes that "psychology in India exists in the twenty-first century in a lifeless form and without impacting debates around individual and political empowerment, rights, or well-being in any significant way" (p. 185).

Notwithstanding this overall assessment, some scholars working within/ against the disciplinary constraints of psychology have centered women's issues in their research. In her review of psychological studies relating to women/gender from 1993–2003 in *Indian Psychological Abstracts and Reviews*, Undurti (2007) observed that there was an increase in such research in the late 1980s. Research that emanated from universities and other academic institutions tended to focus on the work-family interface among urban, educated women and did not generally employ the critical or structural analysis that was characteristic of women's studies. Research emanating from women's advocacy groups tended to focus on women's mental health and violence against women, and tended to employ a critical, structural analysis. As an example, research on domestic violence has tended to focus on the interaction between a culture of male entitlement, the widespread acceptance of violence as endemic to marital relations, family structures (including the role of female kin such as mothers-in-law), and individual personality factors.

Undurti (2007) attributes the academic preponderance of studies on the work-family interface among urban educated women to sampling bias among academics, in which they study the kinds of participants and experiences to which they have access and familiarity. This severely limits the full-spectrum consideration of caste and class, and may downplay the extent to which the cultural valorization of women's roles as mothers and wives may conflict with their roles as workers.

Somewhat more recently, and outside the strict disciplinary purview of psychology, a body of work that examines the impact of globalization on the patterns of life, social and family structures, and economic organization in India has emerged. One of the most tangible and impactful effects of globalization has been the burgeoning of a massive call-center industry, an industry that has intentionally attracted and employed a large number of women (see Basi, 2009; Patel, 2010). The effects of this substantial shift in women's lives and status, and its repercussions throughout Indian society, have begun to be studied by psychologists.

Bhatia (2018), for example, in his larger work on globalization and Indian youth identities, explores the narratives of young women as they navigate their new-found status as significant breadwinners and independent agents while remaining under the control of patriarchal, conservative cultural expectations and attitudes. These attitudes set up a binary of Indian women as either being liberated *or* traditional, with "liberated" synonymous with bad character, dishonor, and promiscuity, and "traditional" equated with decency, modesty, and family orientation. Bhatia describes the strategic identity negotiations that some young women make in response to this complex cultural positioning, in which they attempt to take advantage of the chance to break away from restrictive gender roles (and earn significant income) while minimizing the social disapproval that such behavior will necessarily entail. He concludes that "Women's work in the call centers demonstrates that globalization is generating new cultural concepts of gender roles and gendered identity that are contradictory, contested, and overlapping" (p. 155). Culture and gender are both dynamic and interactive.

6 Conclusion: Gender and/in/as Culture

At the beginning of this Element, I noted that "Culture is in gender, and gender is in culture." That is, one cannot adequately study and understand gender without situating it in culture, and one cannot adequately understand culture without examining how gender is constituted and functions within it. If there are any universals in this story, it is that gender exists everywhere: There are no genderless cultures or cultures in which gender carries no meaning. However, the meanings that gender assumes vary intricately by context, and they change over time, place, and even within persons. This is why a culturally situated analysis of gender is central to generating a relevant and meaningful psychology of gender.

As I have also demonstrated, feminist theory and critique have been an important influence on psychology. These intellectual developments have unfolded within the context of political movements, such as the women's movement, that have themselves had different culturally situated agendas and aims. As a result, feminist psychologies – or psychologies concerned with connecting the study of gender with social justice aims – take different, contextually specific forms.

Throughout, I have also demonstrated, as have many of the theorists discussed here, that one cannot adequately understand gender and/in/as culture without taking history into account. These relationships have always been historically contingent and heavily impacted by both local and global flows of power as they have unfolded over time. The co-constitution of gender and culture is a dynamic and unfolding process but also bears the indelible imprint of historic legacies of colonialism that operate both within and among contemporary nation-states and geopolitical regions. The challenge is to develop psychologies of gender that can incorporate the complexity of these historical, cultural, and political processes while also remaining liberatory in their aims and visions.

References

Adams G., Kurtiş, T., Salter, P. S., & Anderson, S. L. (2012). A cultural psychology of relationship: Decolonizing science and practice. In O. Gillath, G. Adams, & A. D. Kunkel (eds.), *Relationship Science: Integrating Evolutionary, Neuroscience, and Sociocultural Approaches* (pp. 49–70). Washington, DC: American Psychological Association.

Adams, G., Estrada-Villalta, S., & Ordóñez, L. H. G. (2018). The modernity/coloniality of being: Hegemonic psychology as intercultural relations. *International Journal of Intercultural Relations*, *62*, 13–22.

Adams, G., & Salter, P. S. (2007). Health psychology in African settings: A cultural psychological analysis. *Journal of Health Psychology*, *12*, 539–551.

Ahmed, K. H. (2012). Finding a jewel: Identity and gendered space in Islamic finance. *Culture & Psychology*, *18*, 542–558.

Amaro, H., & Russo, N. F. (1987). Hispanic women and mental health: An overview of contemporary issues in research and practice. *Psychology of Women Quarterly*, *11*, 393–407.

Amponsah, B., & Krekling, S. (1997). Sex differences in visual-spatial performance among Ghanaian and Norwegian adults. *Journal of Cross-Cultural Psychology*, *28*, 81–92.

Anzaldua, G. (1987). *Borderlands/La Frontera: The New Mestiza*. San Francisco: aunt lute books.

Basi, T. J. K. (2009). *Women, Identity, and India's Call Center Industry*. London, UK: Routledge.

Bem, S. L. (1974). The measurement of psychological androgyny. *Journal of Consulting and Clinical Psychology*, *42*, 155–162.

Bem, S. L. (1981). Gender schema theory: A cognitive account of sex typing. *Psychological Review*, *88*, 354–364.

Berry, J. W. (2019). *Acculturation: A Personal Journey across Cultures*. Cambridge: Cambridge University Press.

Best, D. L., & Everett, B. S. (2010). The most recent years: *The Journal of Cross-Cultural Psychology*, 2004–2009. *Journal of Cross-Cultural Psychology*, *41*, 329–335.

Best, D. L., & Puzio, A. R. (2019). Gender and culture. In D. Matsumoto & H. C. Hwang (eds.), *The Handbook of Culture and Psychology* (pp. 235–291). New York: Oxford University Press.

Bhabha, H. (1994). *The Location of Culture*. New York: Routledge.

Bhatia, S. (2002). Acculturation, dialogical voices and the construction of the diasporic self. *Theory and Psychology*, *12*, 55–77.

Bhatia, S. (2007). Opening up cultural psychology: Analyzing race, caste, and migrant identities. *Human Development*, *50*, 320–327.

Bhatia, S. (2008). Rethinking culture and identity in psychology: Towards a transnational cultural psychology. *Journal of Theoretical and Philosophical Psychology*, *28*, 301–321.

Bhatia, S. (2018). *Decolonizing Psychology: Globalization, Social Justice, and Indian Youth Identities*. New York: Oxford.

Bhatia, S., & Ram, A. (2001). Rethinking "acculturation" in relation to diasporic cultures and postcolonial identities. *Human Development*, *44*, 1–18.

Bhatia, S., & Ram, A. (2004). Culture, hybridity, and the dialogical self: Cases from the South Asian diaspora. *Mind, Culture, and Activity*, *11*, 224–240.

Boonzaier, F., Kessi, S., & Ravn, A. (2019). Editorial: Psychology and society in dialogue with decolonial feminisms: Perspectives from the global South, Volume 1. *Psychology in Society*, *58*, 1–3.

Bowleg, L. (2008). When Black + lesbian + woman ≠ Black lesbian woman: The methodological challenges of qualitative and quantitative intersectionality research. *Sex Roles 59*, 312–325.

Broverman, I. K., Broverman, D. M., Clarkson, F. E., Rosenkrantz, P. S., & Vogel, S. R. (1970). Sex role stereotypes and clinical judgments of mental health. *Journal of Consulting and Clinical Psychology*, *34*, 1–7.

Brown, L. S. (1995). Cultural diversity in feminist therapy: Theory and practice. In H. Landrine (ed.), *Bringing Cultural Diversity to Feminist Psychology: Theory, Research, and Practice* (pp. 143–162). Washington, DC: American Psychological Association.

Buchanan, N. T., & Ormerod, A. J. (2002). Racialized sexual harassment in the lives of African American women. *Women & Therapy*, *25*, 107–124.

Buchanan, N. T., Rios, D., & Case, K. A. (2020). Intersectional cultural humility: Aligning critical inquiry with critical praxis in psychology. *Women and Therapy*, *43*, 235–243.

Butler, J. (1990). *Gender Trouble: Feminism and the Subversion of Identity*. London, EN: Routledge.

Caplan, P. J. (1985). *The Myth of Women's Masochism*. New York, NY: New American Library.

Chen, X. F., & Cheung, F. (2011). Feminist psychology in China. In A. Rutherford, R. Capdevila, V. Undurti, & I. Palmary (eds.), *Handbook of International Feminisms: Perspectives on Psychology, Women, Culture, and Rights* (pp. 269–292). New York: Springer SBM.

Chesler, P. (1972). *Women and Madness*. Garden City, NY: Doubleday.

Chrisler, J. C., de las Fuentes, C., Durvasula, R. S., Esnil, E. M., McHugh, M.C., Miles-Cohen, S. E., Williams, J. L., & Wisdom, J.P. (2013). The American Psychological Association's Committee on Women in Psychology: 40 years of contributions to the transformation of psychology. *Psychology of Women Quarterly, 37*, 444–454.

Chrisler, J. C., & McHugh, M. C. (2011). Waves of feminist psychology in the United States: Politics and perspectives. In A. Rutherford, R. Capdevila, V. Undurti, & I. Palmary (eds.), *Handbook of International Feminisms: Perspectives on Psychology, Women, Culture, and Rights* (pp. 37–58). New York: Springer Science + Business Media.

Cole, E. R. (2008). Coalitions as a model for intersectionality: From practice to theory. *Sex Roles, 59* (5–6), 443–453.

Cole, E. R., & Stewart, A. J. (2001). Invidious comparisons: Imagining a psychology of race and gender beyond differences. *Political Psychology, 22*(2), 293–308.

Collins, P. H. (1990). *Black Feminist Thought: Knowledge, Consciousness, and the Politics of Empowerment*. New York: Routledge.

Comas-Díaz, L. (1987). Feminist therapy with mainland Puerto Rican women. *Psychology of Women Quarterly, 11*, 461–474.

Comas-Díaz, L. (1991). Feminism and diversity in psychology: The case of women of color. *Psychology of Women Quarterly, 15*, 597–609.

Combahee River Collective (1978). A Black feminist statement. In Z. R. Eisenstein (ed.), *Capitalist Patriarchy and the Case for Socialist Feminism* (pp. 362–372). New York: Monthly Review Press.

Constantinople, A. (1973). Masculinity-femininity: An exception to a famous dictum? *Psychological Bulletin, 80*, 389–407.

Cooper, B. (2016). Intersectionality. In L. Disch & M. Hawkesworth (eds.), *The Oxford Handbook of Feminist Theory* (pp. 385–406). New York: Oxford.

Crawford, M., & Marecek, J. (1989). Psychology reconstructs the female, 1968–1988. *Psychology of Women Quarterly, 13*, 147–166.

Crenshaw, K. (1989). Demarginalizing the intersection of race and sex: A Black feminist critique of antidiscrimination doctrine, feminist theory and antiracist politics. *University of Chicago Legal Forum, 1989*(1), 139–167.

Cretchley, J., Rooney, D., & Gallois, C. (2010). Mapping a 40-year history with Leximancer: Themes and concepts. *Journal of Cross-Cultural Psychology, 41*, 318–328.

De Beauvoir, S. (1949). *The Second Sex*. New York: Vintage Books.

Dill, B. T. (1983). Race, class, and gender: Prospects for an all-inclusive sisterhood. *Feminist Studies, 9*, 131–150.

Dodd, J. (2015). "The name game": Feminist protests of the DSM and diagnostic labels in the 1980s. *History of Psychology, 18*, 312–323.

Ellis, B., & Stam, H. (2015). Crisis? What crisis? Cross-cultural psychology's appropriation of cultural psychology. *Culture & Psychology, 21*, 293–317.

Espín, O. (1987). Psychological impact of migration on Latinas: Implications for psychotherapeutic practice. *Psychology of Women Quarterly, 11*, 489–503.

Espín, O. (1999). *Women Crossing Boundaries: The Psychology of Immigration and the Transformations of Sexuality*. New York: Routledge.

Espín, O. (2006). Gender, sexuality, language, and migration. In R. Mahalingam (ed.), *Cultural Psychology of Immigrants* (pp. 241–258). Mahwah, NJ: Lawrence Erlbaum.

Fausto-Sterling, A. (2000). *Sexing the Body: Gender Politics and the Construction of Sexuality*. New York: Basic Books.

Fausto-Sterling, A. (2012). *Sex/Gender*. New York: Routledge.

Fine, M. (2018). *Just Research in Contentious Times: Widening the Methodological Imagination*. New York: Teachers College Press.

Fine, M., & Ruglis, J. (2009). Circuits and consequences of dispossession: The racialized realignment of the public sphere for US youth. *Transforming Anthropology, 17*, 20–33.

Findlay, D. (1995). Discovering sex: Medical science, feminist, and intersexuality. *The Canadian Review of Sociology and Anthropology, 32*, 25–52.

Gavey, N. (1989). Feminist poststructuralism and discourse analysis: Contributions to feminist psychology. *Psychology of Women Quarterly, 13*, 459–475.

George, M. L. (2012). Profile of Martha Bernal. In A. Rutherford (ed.), *Psychology's Feminist Voices Multimedia Internet Archive*. www .feministvoices.com/martha-bernal

Gergen, M. (2001). *Feminist Reconstructions in Psychology. Narrative, Gender, and Performance*. Thousand Oaks, CA: Sage.

Gergen, K. J. (2011). The self as a social construction. *Psychological Studies, 56*, 108–116.

Germon, J. (2009). *Gender: A Genealogy of an Idea*. New York: Palgrave Macmillan.

Gilligan, C. (1982). *In a Different Voice*. Cambridge, MA: Harvard University Press.

Grabe, S., & Dutt, A. (2015). Counter-narratives, the psychology of liberation, and the evolution of a women's social movement in Nicaragua. *Peace and Conflict: Journal of Peace Psychology, 21*, 89–105.

Grabe, S., & Else-Quest, N. S. (2012). The role of transnational feminism in psychology: Complementary visions. *Psychology of Women Quarterly, 36,* 158–161.

Grosz, E. (1994). *Volatile Bodies: Towards a Corporeal Feminism.* Bloomington: Indiana University Press.

Grzanka, P. (2020). From buzzword to critical psychology: An invitation to take intersectionality seriously. *Women & Therapy, 43,* 244–261.

Hancock, A. (2011). *Solidarity Politics for Millennials: A Guide to Ending the Oppression Olympics.* New York: Springer.

Hancock, A. (2016). *Intersectionality: An Intellectual History.* New York: Oxford.

Hermans, H. J. M., & Kempen, H. J. G. (1998). Moving cultures: The perilous problems of cultural dichotomies in a globalizing society. *American Psychologist, 53,* 1111–1120.

Hobbs, A. (2014). *A Chosen Exile: A History of Racial Passing in American Life.* Cambridge, MA: Harvard University Press.

hooks, b. (1981). *Ain't I a Woman? Black Women and Feminism.* Boston: South End Press.

hooks, b. (1984). *Feminist Theory: From Margin to Center.* Boston: South End Press.

Hurtado, A. (1997). *The Color of Privilege: Three Blasphemies on Race and Feminism.* Ann Arbor: The University of Michigan Press.

Hutz, C. S., Gauert, G., & Gomes, W. B. (2012). Brazil. In D. Baker (ed.), *The Oxford Handbook of the History of Psychology: Global Perspectives* (pp. 34–50).

Hyde, J. S. (2005). The gender similarities hypothesis. *American Psychologist, 60,* 581–592.

Hyde, J. S., Bigler, R., Joel, D., Tate, C. , & van Anders, S. (2019). The future of sex and gender in psychology: Five challenges to the gender binary. *American Psychologist, 74,* 171–193.

Hyde, J. S., & Rosenberg, B. G. (1976). *Half the Human Experience: The Psychology of Women.* Lexington: D. C. Heath.

Jack, D. C. (1991). *Silencing the Self: Women and Sepression.* Cambridge, MA: Harvard University Press.

Kashima, Y., & Gelfand, M. J. (2012). A history of culture in psychology. In A. W. Kruglanski & W. Stroebe (eds.), *Handbook of the History of Social Psychology* (pp. 499–520). New York: Psychology Press.

Keith, K. (2008). Cross-cultural psychology and research. In S. F. Davis & W. Buskist (eds.), *21st Century Psychology: A Research Handbook, Volume 2* (pp. 483–490). Thousand Oaks, CA: Sage.

Keith, K. D. (ed.) (2019). *Cross-Cultural Psychology: Contemporary Themes and Perspectives*, 2nd ed. New York: Wiley.

Keller, E. F. (1985). *Reflections on Gender and Science*. New Haven and London: Yale University Press.

Kessler, S., & McKenna, S. (1978). *Gender: An Ethnomethodological Approach*. New York: Wiley.

Kim, S., & Rutherford, A. (2015). From seduction to sexism: Feminists challenge the ethics of therapist-client sexual relations in 1970s America. *History of Psychology, 18*(3), 283–296.

Kirmayer, L. J. (2012). Rethinking cultural competence. *Transcultural Psychiatry, 49*, 149–164.

Kirschner, S. R., & Martin, J. (eds.) (2010). *The Sociocultural Turn in Psychology*. New York: Columbia University Press.

Kite, M. E., Togans, L. J., & Schultz, T. J. (2019). Stability or change? A cross-cultural look at attitudes toward sexual and gender minorities. In K. Keith (ed.), *Cross-Cultural Psychology: Contemporary Themes and Perspectives,* 2nd ed. (pp. 427–448). New York: Wiley.

Kitzinger, C. (1994). Should psychologists study sex differences? *Feminism & Psychology, 4*, 501–546.

Klein, V. (1946). *The Feminine Character: History of an Ideology*. London: Routledge and Kegan Paul Ltd.

Kleinman, A., & Benson, P. (2006). Anthropology in the clinic: The problem of cultural competency and how to fix it. *PLoS Medicine, 3* (10), e294, 1673–1676.

Kumar, M. (2006). Rethinking psychology in India: Debating294 pasts and futures. *Annual Review of Critical Psychology*, 5, 236–256.

Kumar, M. (2011). (Re)locating the feminist standpoint in the practice of psychology today: The case of India. In A. Rutherford, R. Capdevila, V. Undurti, & I. Palmary (eds.), *Handbook of International Feminisms: Perspectives on Psychology, Women, Culture, and Rights* (pp. 175–194). New York: Springer SBM.

Kuper, A. (1999). *Culture: The Anthropologists' Account*. Cambridge, MA: Harvard University Press.

Kurtiş, T. (2010). Self-silencing and well-being among Turkish women (Unpublished master's thesis). University of Kansas, Lawrence, KS.

Kurtiş, T., & Adams, G. (2015). Decolonizing liberation: Toward a transnational feminist psychology. *Journal of Social and Political Psychology, 3*, 388–413.

Kurtiş, T., & Adams, G. (2017). Decolonial intersectionality: Implications for theory, research, and pedagogy. In K. Case (ed.), *Intersectional Pedagogy: Complicating Identity and Social Justice* (pp. 46–59). New York: Routledge.

Laqueur, T. (1990). *Making Sex: Body and Gender from the Greeks to Freud*. Cambridge, MA: Harvard University Press.

Lips, H. M., & Lawson, K. M. (2019). Women across cultures. In K. Keith (ed.), *Cross-Cultural Psychology: Contemporary Themes and Perspectives,* 2nd ed. (pp. 401–426). New York: Wiley.

Lonner, W. (2013). Chronological benchmarks in cross-cultural psychology. Foreword to the *Encyclopedia of Cross-Cultural Psychology. Online Readings in Psychology and Culture, 1* (2). https://doi.org/10.9707/2307–0919.1124

Lugones, M. (2010). Toward a decolonial feminism. *Hypatia, 25,* 742–759.

Maccoby, E. E., & Jacklin, C. N. (1974). *The Psychology of Sex Differences*. Stanford, CA: Stanford University Press.

Macleod, C., Bhatia, S., & Liu, W. (2020). Feminisms and decolinising psychology: Possibilities and challenges. *Feminism & Psychology, 30,* 287–305.

Macleod, C., Masuko, D., & Feltham-King, T. (2019). Why decolonialising feminist psychology may fail, and why it mustn't: The politics of signification and the case of "teenage pregnancy." *Psychology in Society, 58,* 50–70.

Madureira, A. F. A. (2012). Belonging to gender: Social identities, symbolic boundaries and images. In J. Valsiner (ed.), *The Handbook of Culture and Psychology* (pp. 582–601). New York: Oxford University Press.

Magnusson, E., & Marecek, J. (2012). *Gender and Culture in Psychology: Theories and Practices*. New York: Cambridge University Press.

Maldonado-Torres, N. (2007). On the coloniality of Being: Contributions to the development of a concept. *Cultural Studies, 21,* 240–270.

Markus, H. R., & Kitayama, S. (1991). Culture and the self: Implications for cognition, emotion, and motivation. *Psychological Review, 98,* 224–253.

Martin, E. (1991). The egg and the sperm: How science has constructed a romance based on stereotypical male-female roles. *Signs,16,* 485–501.

Mays, V., & Comas-Díaz, L. (1988). Feminist therapy with ethnic minority populations: A closer look at Blacks and Hispanics. In M. A. Dutton-Douglas & L. A. Walkjer (eds.), *Feminist Psychotherapies: Integration of Therapeutic and Feminist Systems* (pp. 228–251). Norwood, NJ: Ablex.

McClintock, A. (1995). *Imperial Leather: Race, Gender, and Sexuality in the Colonial Contest*. New York: Routledge.

McCrae, R. R., Costa, P. T., Pilar, G. H., Rolland, J.P., & Parker, W. D. (1998). Cross-cultural assessment of the five-factor model: The revised NEO personality inventory. *Journal of Cross-Cultural Psychology, 29*, 171–188.

Mead, M. (1935). *Sex and Temperament in Three Primitive Societies.* New York: New American Library.

Mendoza, B. (2016). Coloniality of gender and power: From postcoloniality to decoloniality. In L. Disch & M. Hawkesworth (eds), *The Oxford Handbook of Feminist Theory* (pp. 100–121). New York: Oxford University Press.

Metzl, J., & Hansen, H. (2014). Structural competency: Theorizing a new medical engagement with stigma and inequality. *Social Science and Medicine, 103*, 126–133.

Meyerowitz, J. (2002). *How Sex Changed: A History of Transsexuality in the United States.* Cambridge, MA: Harvard University Press.

Mignolo, W. (2011). *The Darker Side of Western Modernity: Global Futures, Decolonial Options.* Durham, NC: Duke University Press.

Misra, G., & Gergen, K. (1993). On the place of culture in psychological science. *International Journal of Psychology, 28*, 225–243.

Moane, G. (1999). *Gender and Colonialism: A Psychological Analysis of Oppression and Liberation.* New York: Palgrave MacMillan.

Mohanty, C. T. (1988). Under Western eyes: Feminist scholarship and colonial discourses. *Feminist Review, 30*, 61–88.

Money, J. (1995). *Gendermaps: Social Constructionism, Feminism, and Sexosophical History.* New York: Continuum.

Morawski, J. G. (1985). The measurement of masculinity and femininity: Engendering categorical realities. *Journal of Personality, 53*, 196–223.

Murray, S. R. (1977, April). Report of the Task Force on Black Women's Priorities, Division 35 Archives, Box 1, Folder 70. American Psychological Association, Washington, DC.

Murray, S. R., & Scott, P. B. (1982). Introduction. *Psychology of Women Quarterly, 6*, 259–260.

Nuernberg, A. H., Toneli, M. J. F., Medrado, B., & Lyra, J. (2011). Feminism, psychology, and gender studies: The Brazilian case. In A. Rutherford, R. Capdevila, V. Undurti, & I. Palmary (eds.), *Handbook of International Feminisms: Perspectives on Psychology, Women, Culture, and Rights* (pp. 109–128). New York: Springer SBM.

Oudshoorn, N. (1994). *Beyond the Natural Body: An Archeology of Sex Hormones.* New York: Routledge.

Patel, R. (2010). *Working the Night Shift: Women in India's Call Center Industry.* Stanford, CA: Stanford University Press.

Patil, V. (2013). From patriarchy to intersectionality: A transnational feminist assessment of how far we've really come. *Signs, 38*, 847–867.

Porter, T., & Schumann, K. (2017). Intellectual humility and openness to the opposing view. *Self and Identity*, 1–24.

Purdie-Vaughns, V., & Eibach, R. P. (2008). Intersectional invisibility: The distinctive advantages and disadvantages of multiple subordinate-group identities. *Sex Roles, 59*, 377–391.

Reid, P.T. (1993). Poor women in psychological research: "Shut up and shut out." *Psychology of Women Quarterly,17*, 133–150.

Reid, P. T., & Comas-Díaz, L. (1990). Gender and ethnicity: Perspectives on dual status. *Sex Roles, 22*, 397–408.

Richardson, S. S. (2013). *Sex Itself: The Search for Male and Female in the Human Genome*. Chicago: University of Chicago Press.

Riggs, D., Pearce, R., Pfeffer, C., Hines, S., White, F., & Ruspini, E. (2019). Transnormativity in the psy-disciplines: Constructing pathology in the *Diagnostic and Statistical Manual of Mental Disorders* and *Standards of Care*. *American Psychologist, 74*, 912–924.

Riley, D. (1988). *Am I That Name? Feminism and the Category of "Women" in History*. New York: Macmillan.

Ross, L. J. (2017). Reproductive justice as intersectional feminist activism. *Souls: A Critical Journal of Black Politics, Culture, and Society, 19*, 286–314.

Rubin, D. A. (2012). "An unnamed blank that craved a name": A genealogy of intersex as gender. *Signs: Journal of Women in Culture and Society, 37*, 883–908.

Russo, N. F. & Dumont, A. (1997). A history of Division 35 (Psychology of women): Origins, issues, activities, future. In D. A. Dewsbury (ed.), *Unification through Division: Histories of the Divisions of the American Psychological Association, Volume 2* (pp. 211–238). Washington, DC: APA.

Rutherford, A. (2007). Feminist questions, feminist answers: Toward a redefinition. *Feminism & Psychology, 17*, 459–464.

Rutherford, A. (2015). Maintaining masculinity in mid-20th century American psychology: Edwin Boring, scientific eminence, and the "woman problem." *Osiris: Scientific Masculinities, 30*, 250–271.

Rutherford, A. (2017). "Making better use of US women": Psychology, sex roles, and womanpower in post-WWII America. *Journal of the History of the Behavioral Sciences, 53*, 228–245.

Rutherford, A. (2019). Gender. In R. Sternberg & W. E. Pickren (eds.), *The Cambridge Handbook of the Intellectual History of Psychology* (pp. 345–370). Cambridge: Cambridge University Press.

Rutherford, A. (2020). Doing science, doing gender: Using history in the present. *Journal of Theoretical and Philosophical Psychology*, *40*, 21–31.

Rutherford, A., Capdevila, R., Undurti, V., & Palmary, I. (eds.) (2011). *Handbook of International Feminisms: Perspectives on Psychology, Women, Culture, and Rights*. New York: Springer SBM.

Rutherford, A., & Granek, L. (2010). Emergence and development of the psychology of women. In J. Chrisler & D. McCreary (eds.), *Handbook of Gender Research in Psychology* (pp. 19–41). New York: Springer.

Rutherford, A., Marecek, J., & Sheese, K. (2012). Psychology of women and gender. In D. K. Freedheim & I. B. Weiner (eds.). *Handbook of Psychology, Volume 1: History of Psychology, 2nd ed.* (pp. 279–301). New York: Wiley.

Rutherford, A., & Pettit, M. (2015). Feminism and/in/as psychology: The public sciences of sex and gender. *History of Psychology*, *18*(3), 223–237.

Rutherford, A., Vaughn-Johnson, K., & Rodkey, E. (2015, June). Does psychology have a gender? *The Psychologist*, *28*(6), 2–4.

Scarborough, E., & Rutherford, A. (2018). Women in the APA. In W. E. Pickren & A. Rutherford (eds.), *125 Years of the American Psychological Association* (pp. 321–357). Washington, DC: APA.

Scott, J. W. (1986). Gender as a useful category of historical analysis. *American Historical Review*, *91*, 1053–1075.

Settles, I. H. (2006). Use of an intersectional framework to understand Black women's racial and gender identities. *Sex Roles*, *54*, 589–601.

Seward, G. H. (1946). *Sex and the Social Order*. New York and London: McGraw-Hill.

Seward, G. H., & Williamson, R. C. (1970). *Sex roles in Changing Society*. New York: Radom House.

Shields, S. A. (2008). Gender: An intersectionality perspective. *Sex Roles*, *59*, 301–311.

Shweder, R. A. (1984). Anthropology's romantic rebellion against the enlightenment, or there's more to thinking than reason and evidence. In R. A. Shweder & R. A. Levine (eds.), *Culture Theory* (pp. 27–66). Cambridge, UK: Cambridge University Press.

Shweder, R. A. (1991). *Thinking through Cultures*. Cambridge, MA: Harvard University Press.

Sieben, A. (2016). Gender in culture-inclusive psychologies: A situated and selective mapping of historical and contemporary territories. *Cultural Psychology*, *22*, 546–564.

Sinha, D. (1986). *Psychology in a Third World Country: The Indian Experience*. Delhi: Sage.

Sinha, D. (1998). Changing perspectives in social psychology in India: A journey towards indigenization. *Asian Journal of Social Psychology, 1,* 17–31.

Slunecko, T., & Wieser, M. (2014). Cultural psychology. In T. Teo (ed.), *Encyclopedia of Critical Psychology* (pp. 347–352). New York: Springer. https://doi.org/ezproxy.library.yorku.ca/10.1007/978-1-4614-5583-7_370

Smith, L. T. (1999). *Decolonizing Methodologies: Research and Indigenous Peoples.* London: Zed Books.

Smye, V., Josewski, V., & Kendall, E. (2010). *Cultural Safety: An Overview.* Ottawa, Canada: First Nations, Inuit and Metis Advisory Committee, Mental Health Commission of Canada.

Spence, J. T., & Helmreich, R. L. (1978). *Masculinity & Femininity: Their Psychological Dimensions, Correlates, and Antecedents.* Austin: University of Texas Press.

Spivak, G. (1985). Three women's texts and a critique of imperialism. *Critical Inquiry, 12,* 243–261.

Spivak, G. C. (1988). Can the subaltern speak? In C. Nelson & L. Grossber (eds.). *Marxism and the Interpretation of Culture* (pp. 271–313). London: Macmillan.

Stack, C. B. (1994). Different voices, different visions: Gender, culture, and moral reasoning. In M. B. Zinn & B. T. Dill (eds.), *Women of Color in US Society* (pp. 291–302). Temple University Press.

Stoler, A. S. (2002). *Carnal Knowledge and Imperial Power: Race and the Intimate in Colonial Rule.* Berkeley, CA: University of California Press.

Stoller, R. (1968). *Sex and Gender: On the Development of Masculinity and Femininity.* London: Karnac Books.

Stryker, S. (2008) *Transgender History.* Seattle, WA: Seal Press.

Tarrant, S. (2006). *When Sex Became Gender.* New York: Routledge.

Tiefer, L. (1991). A brief history of the Association for Women in Psychology, 1969–1991. *Psychology of Women Quarterly, 15,* 635–649.

Tonks R. G. (2014). Cross-cultural psychology, Overview. In T. Teo (ed.), *Encyclopedia of Critical Psychology* (pp. 334–341). New York: Springer. https://doi.org/ezproxy.library.yorku.ca/10.1007/978-1-4614-5583-7_370

Undurti, V. (2007). Quality of women's lives in India: Some findings from two decades of psychological research on gender. *Feminism & Psychology, 17,* 337–356. (mistakenly published as Vindhya, U.)

Unger, R. K. (1979). Toward a redefinition of sex and gender. *American Psychologist, 34,* 1085–1094.

Unger, R. K. (2010). Leave no text behind: Teaching the psychology of women during the emergence of second wave feminism. *Sex Roles, 62,* 153–158.

van Anders, S. M. (2015). Beyond sexual orientation: Integrating gender/sex and diverse sexualities via sexual configurations theory. *Archives of Sexual Behavior, 44*, 1177–1213.

Viveras-Vigoya, M. V. (2016). Sex/gender. In L. Disch & M. Hawkesworth (eds), *The Oxford Handbook of Feminist Theory* (pp. 852–873). New York: Oxford University Press.

Warner, L., Kurtiş, T., & Adya, A. (2020). Navigating criticisms of intersectional approaches: Reclaiming intersectionality for global social justice and well-being. *Women & Therapy, 43*, 262–277.

Weis, L., & Fine, M. (2012, summer). Critical bifocality and circuits of privilege. *Harvard Educational Review, 82*, 173–201.

Weisstein, N. (1971). Psychology constructs the female; or, the fantasy life of the male psychologist (with some attention to the fantasies of his friends, the male biologist and the male anthropologist). *Journal of Social Education, 35*, 362–373.

West, C., & Zimmerman, D. H. (1987). Doing gender. *Gender and Society, 1*, 125–161.

Whitcomb, D., Battaly, H., Baehr, J., & Howard-Snyder, D. (2017). Intellectual humility: Owning our limitations. *Philosophy and Phenomenological Research, 94*(3), 509–539.

Wilson, E. A. (2004). *Psychosomatic: Feminism and the Neurological Body.* Durham, NC: Duke University Press.

Cambridge Elements ☰

Psychology and Culture

Kenneth D. Keith

University of San Diego

Kenneth D. Keith is author or editor of more than 160 publications on cross-cultural psychology, quality of life, intellectual disability, and the teaching of psychology. He was the 2017 president of the Society for the Teaching of Psychology.

About the Series

Elements in Psychology and Culture features authoritative surveys and updates on key topics in cultural, cross-cultural, and indigenous psychology. Authors are internationally recognized scholars whose work is at the forefront of their subdisciplines within the realm of psychology and culture.

Cambridge Elements ☰

Psychology and Culture

Printed in the United States
By Bookmasters